THE LANGUAGE OF LITERATURE

'This is the series we've all been waiting for! Tightly focused on the assessment objectives, these books provide an excellent aid to classroom teaching and self-study. Whether your school changes board or text, or decides to offer Literature and/or Language to 6th formers these books are still the tool that can make a real difference to results.'

Emmeline McChleery, Aylesford School, Warwick

Routledge A Level English Guides equip AS and A2 Level students with the skills they need to explore, evaluate, and enjoy English. What has – until now – been lacking for the revised English A Levels is a set of textbooks that equip students with the concepts, skills and knowledge they need to succeed in light of the way the exams are actually working. The *Routledge A Level English Guides* series fills this critical gap.

Books in the series are built around the various skills specified in the assessment objectives (AOs) for all AS and A2 Level English courses, and take into account how these AOs are being interpreted by the exam boards. Focusing on the AOs most relevant to their topic, the books help students to develop their knowledge and abilities through analysis of a wide range of texts and data. Each book also offers accessible **explanations**, **examples**, **exercises**, **suggested answers** and **a glossary of key terms**.

The series helps students to learn what is required of them and develop skills accordingly, while ensuring that English remains an exciting subject that students enjoy studying. The books are also an essential resource for teachers trying to create lessons which balance the demands of the exam boards with the more general skills and knowledge students need for the critical appreciation of English Language and Literature.

ROUTLEDGE A LEVEL ENGLISH GUIDES

About the Series Editor

Adrian Beard was Head of English at Gosforth High School, Newcastle upon Tyne. He now works at the University of Newcastle upon Tyne and is a Chief Examiner for AS and A2 Level English Literature. He is co-series editor of the Routledge Intertext series, and his publications include *Texts and Contexts*, *The Language of Politics*, and *The Language of Sport* (all for Routledge).

TITLES IN THE SERIES

The Language of Literature
Adrian Beard

How Texts Work
Adrian Beard

Language and Social Contexts
Amanda Coultas

Writing for Assessment
Angela Goddard

Transforming Texts
Shaun O'Toole

THE LANGUAGE OF LITERATURE

Adrian Beard

Routledge
Taylor & Francis Group

LONDON AND NEW YORK

First published 2003
by Routledge
11 New Fetter Lane, London EC4P 4EE

Simultaneously published in the USA and Canada
by Routledge
29 West 35th Street, New York, NY 10001

Routledge is an imprint of the Taylor & Francis Group

Typeset in Galliard by Keystroke, Jacaranda Lodge, Wolverhampton
Printed and bound in Great Britain by TJ International Ltd, Padstow, Cornwall

British Library Cataloguing in Publication Data
A catalogue record for this book is available from the British Library

Library of Congress Cataloging in Publication Data
A catalog record for this book has been requested

ISBN 0–415–28632–8 (hbk)
ISBN 0–415–28633–6 (pbk)

CONTENTS

PREFACE

ASSESSMENT OBJECTIVES

The AS/A2 specifications in English are governed by assessment objectives (or AOs) which break down each of the subjects into component parts and skills. These assessment objectives have been used to create the different modules which together form a sort of a jigsaw puzzle. Different objectives are highlighted in different modules, but at the end of AS and again at the end of A2 each of the objectives has been given a roughly equal weighting.

The function of language that will be focused on in this book is how it is used in the creation of literary texts. That said, many students find writing about the language of literature difficult. It is one thing to comment on what was written about, quite another to write about how it was written. This book will help you to analyse literary texts by looking at the ways in which language has been used in their formation.

Each chapter contains a number of exercises. When the exercise introduces a new idea, there will usually be suggestions for answer immediately following. When the exercise checks to see if a point has been understood, suggestions for answer can be found at the end of the book.

See overleaf for assessment objectives that are focused on in this book.

English Literature

AO1: In writing about literary texts, you must use appropriate terminology.

AO2: You must show knowledge and understanding of literary texts of different types and periods, exploring and commenting on relationships and comparisons between literary texts.

AO3: You must show how writers' choices of form, structure and language shape meanings.

AO4: You must provide independent opinions and judgements, informed by different interpretations by other readers of literary texts.

AO5: You must look at contextual factors which affect the way texts are written, read and understood.

English Language and Literature

AO1: You must show knowledge and understanding of texts gained from the combined study of literary and non-literary texts.

AO2: In responding to literary and non-literary texts, you must distinguish, describe and interpret variation in meaning and form.

AO3: You must respond to and analyse texts, using literary and linguistic concepts and approaches.

AO4: You must show understanding of the ways contextual variation and choices of form, style and vocabulary shape the meanings of texts.

AO5: You must consider the ways attitudes and values are created and conveyed in speech and writing.

English Language

AO1: In writing about texts, you must use appropriate terminology.

AO3: You must show a systematic approach to analysing texts.

AO5: You must analyse the ways contextual factors affect the way texts are written, read and understood.

ACKNOWLEDGEMENTS

Edwin Morgan, 'Centaur', in *Collected Poems*, © Carcanet Press Ltd, 1996.
Alison Lurie, *The Last Resort*, published by Chatto & Windus. Reprinted by permission of The Random House Group Ltd., 1998.
Steven Berkoff, *West*, from *Collected Plays I*, © Faber & Faber Ltd., 1973.

STARTING POINTS   CHAPTER 1

This opening chapter will outline different aspects of literary language and look at the ways in which examination questions ask for the analysis of literary language. It will then introduce some of the main ideas in this book by exploring a short poem by Pope, plus two poems by Blake.

IDENTIFYING THE TASK

The first important point is to identify where you are being asked to analyse language in an exam question, and that instruction can come in a number of different forms. All of the following are used in exam questions, and all require language analysis in the answer.

The How Questions

The word 'how' should immediately alert you to the fact that the author's method is under review. Here are some typical configurations using this keyword. Replace the word 'author' with an actual name if you are studying set texts:

How does (the author) present . . . ?
How is (the author's) attitude to . . . revealed?
How does (the author) use language here?
How does (the author) communicate the significance of . . . ?

The Science Metaphors

Another way of indicating the requirement to look at language is to give an instruction at the beginning of the task, rather than asking a question. Here are some examples.

Examine the ways in which (the author) . . .
Explore the ways in which (the author) . . .
Look at (the author's) handling of . . .
Discuss (the author's) presentation of . . .
Comment on (the author's) use of . . .

There are two things to note here. The first is the way that the imperative verbs, such as 'examine', 'explore', are often scientific metaphors of dissection and discovery. The second is that there are a number of terms which refer to an author's method, such as 'ways in which', 'handling of', 'presentation of', 'use of'.

Some of the tasks above ask you metaphorically to be a scientist, to explore and examine like a doctor would. It's unlikely, though, that you would let someone explore and examine you if they confessed to having no method of enquiry and no experience. Commenting on literary language requires having a method, a method that is refined through practice.

HAVING A METHOD

The first and most important point about analysing literary language is that it should not be done in a vacuum. Do not isolate the language from everything else that is going on. Meanings and language work together, not separately. So, for example, you may well be aware that a text can be seen to belong to the time in which it was written, and to have links with other texts, but it also needs a response from you as a contemporary reader. In other words, looking at language will also involve looking at **context**. (For further ideas about context, see *Texts and Contexts* by Adrian Beard also published by Routledge.)

The following broad categories are helpful as starting points to thinking about literary language and each of them will be looked at in more detail during this book. They are inevitably fairly crude divisions, and will often overlap, but they are useful in identifying possible areas to look at when answering the question 'how'.

---

1. **Genre:** Look for how whole texts fit into genres, how texts relate to other texts. Consider genre in terms of its shape/form, and in terms of its content. Consider the ways in which genre can be subverted, by mixing, for example, inappropriate content and form.
2. **Shapes and patterns:** Look for titles, openings and closings, the connections between parts of the text. Look also at patterns of repeated words, repeated sounds (alliteration, assonance, rhyme, etc.), repeated **grammar** structures, semantic fields (i.e. words which cluster around the same area of meaning).
3. **Narrative:** Look for the voices which 'speak' the texts, how much they know, their reliability, shifting narrators, the role of the reader in identifying narrative point of view, irony.
4. **Voices in texts:** Look for the voices which speak in texts such as characters in drama, dialogue in novels. Consider the use of different levels of formality, regional speech and so on.
5. **Creativity and play:** Look for metaphors and comparisons and work out what they contribute to meanings. Look for multiple meanings and how they are created. Look for ways in which authors use language creatively such as by using archaic words, inventing 'new' words, breaking grammatical rules, using unusual

graphology, playing with words and meanings, creating ambiguity, suggesting absence – what is not in the text but might be expected to be, making intertextual references.

The chapters in this book look at each of these topics in turn.

Exercise 1

The poem below, by Alexander Pope, is a useful starting point for putting some of these early ideas into practice. The following question is typical of the wording you might find in an exam:

How do the form and language of this poem contribute to its effect on the reader?

In order to help you break down the question into some important categories, make notes on these points:

- Research the term epigram – what expectations of an epigram do readers have? **(Genre)**
- What might be the significance of the poem's title? **(Shapes and patterns)**
- Find examples of repetition, variation and contrast in this poem. **(Shapes and patterns)**
- What is the role of the **narrative voice** or voices which are either heard or implied in this poem? **(Narrative)**
- What point is the poem making?

> ### Epigram from the French
>
> Sir, I admit your gen'ral rule
> That every poet is a fool:
> But you yourself may serve to show it,
> That every fool is not a poet.
> Alexander Pope (1732)

Suggestions for Answer

There is no point in talking about language if you ignore what the overall purpose of the language is. Before looking at this poem's structure, then, we need to say briefly what the poem seems to be about. Then, having looked at the poem's structure we will be in a position to refine those ideas about the poem's meanings.

In this poem Pope admits to an unnamed 'Sir' that as a general rule all poets are fools, but then adds that while poets may all be fools, all fools aren't poets. In other words, being a poet and a fool is preferable to being a fool and nothing else.

All titles of texts are significant and are worth considering, not least because writers themselves usually give lots of thought to how they label their work. In this case the title tells us that the poem belongs to a certain genre – it is an epigram – and so experienced readers, who know about epigrams, will have a certain sense of what to expect. This sense of genre is an important one when thinking about structure. Just as buildings reflect other similar buildings in shape and purpose, so literary texts, while unique in some ways, are at the same time similar to other texts. Another way of describing this is to say that all texts in some way have **intertextual** links with other texts, and one way to think about such intertextual links is through reference to genre. In this poem, therefore, Pope signals in his title by using the word 'epigram' that he has written a short rhyming poem which will have some sort of satirical content.

The rest of the title is more puzzling, though. 'From the French' may simply mean that the poem is a translation, or it may have a more specific reference that is not available to us as modern readers. This sense of uncertainty is not necessarily a bad thing, and showing an awareness of significance that is not fully clear will still be rewarded in exams.

So far, then, we have looked at the title of the poem, which has signalled very specifically what genre this poem belongs to. At the end of the poem we are given the poet's name and a date. In terms of the text's context these may be useful, depending on what we already know and what we can research. For our purposes here it is enough to say that Pope is known as a satirical poet; many of his poems make moral comments about the behaviour of humans in general, or his enemies in particular – and he was a man with plenty of enemies.

Now that we have looked at some of the external structures, we can look at some of the more intricate details. Because this is an epigram, a short poem, we will be looking at precise detail, but the principles involved would be the same if we were looking at much longer texts. Seeing how the parts relate to each other and where the author has put emphasis are key aspects of looking at structure.

This poem is built on repetition and variation, as many poems are. The repetition comes in a number of ways: it involves the repetition of actual words, the repetition of grammatical units and the repetition of sound. The repetition of sound is made up of two parts: rhythm and rhyme. The rhythm of the poem involves a considerable number of stresses. In the first line, for example, the first three syllables are all stressed. In a poem made up of two rhyming couplets we would expect each line to end with a strongly stressed syllable. In the first two lines that is indeed the case, with 'rule' rhyming with 'fool'. In the second pair of lines, though, Pope has a variation. This time the rhyme involves two syllables – 'show it' and 'poet' – with the stress falling on the first of the two syllables. In a poem where Pope is suggesting that he may be a fool, but at least a clever one, it seems natural that he should make a 'clever' rhyme to cement his point.

Repetition works alongside contrast in this poem, contrast being another form of repetition. So, while the words 'poet' and 'fool' appear in the second and last lines, each time preceded by 'That every', there is a reversal in the word order. Another form of repetition comes in the use of pronouns. Although the second word in lines one and three is a pronoun, there is a very important contrast between 'I' in line one and 'you' in line three. What the poem has, then, is two pairs of rhyming couplets, with the second pair echoing the first pair, yet at the same time subtly changing it. This sense of the two pairs of lines being separate yet connected is signalled by two things. The first is a piece of punctuation, the colon, which shows a shift of emphasis, yet at the same time a connection to what has gone before. The same effect is created with the **connective** 'But': as a connective it is clearly signalling a connection, yet in its meaning it signals separation and difference. The whole structure of the poem pivots on the colon and the connective 'But'.

In the section on narrative later in this book you will find a detailed examination of the ways in which texts contain 'voices'. The point to make here is that the voices created in texts are a vital part of the overall structure; they act as a sort of foundation upon which the text is built. Here there are two voices in evidence, the voice which narrates the poem and the voice which is reported.

The **narrative voice**, the 'I' of the poem, is not necessarily Pope himself – indeed it can be argued that even in highly personal writing, the very act of writing means that a new character is being created. It helps, therefore, to use the term **narrative persona** to describe the 'I' of a text. Even though Pope is a poet, and this is a poem which is in part about poetry and poets, this does not mean we should lose sight of the fact that Pope, rather like a dramatist, creates a voice within this poem. This is immediately evident with the formal address to 'Sir'. We do not know who this 'Sir' is, certainly not from the distance of nearly three hundred years, but as with the persona we do not have to assume that it is a 'real' person.

Given that the poem goes on to say that the person being addressed is a fool, the created voice is less polite and formal than it may initially seem. The elegant construction of the poem, through its patterns and shape, belies a much more cutting and sarcastic edge. This would have been more clearly seen by Pope's contemporaries than by modern readers, for whom the word 'fool' suggests a relatively light, even affectionate criticism. In Pope's time, though, the word, derived from the French(!) for madness also had connotations of a jester, of a hired entertainer kept in large houses to entertain guests. Taking this sense of the word 'fool' into account, poets with their paying sponsors, and fools with their 'owners', were indeed doing much the same job.

The second voice is only reported, but is still important. The 'Sir' addressed is clearly a man of opinions, a man fond of making 'gen'ral rule(s)'. There is a strong sense that this man has power and self-importance, but these qualities are undermined by the more dominant voice which narrates the poem.

The following ideas, then, have been looked at in the analysis of Pope's 'Epigram from the French':

- The significance of genre in terms of the experienced reader's expectations of a text's shape and purpose
- The significance of external features of form such as the poem's title
- The potential significance of context, with regard to such things as what is already known about an author, his previous works and/or the time of writing
- The significance of repetition, variation and contrast. In the case of this poem, the repetition works through repeated patterns of words, sounds and grammar – and contrasting variations of these
- The role of the narrative voice or voices either heard or implied in a text

Exercise 2

Taking into account what has been looked at so far, this chapter now looks at two linked poems by William Blake.

Nurse's Song

When the voices of children are heard on the green
And laughing is heard on the hill,
My heart is at rest within my breast
And everything else is still.

'Then come my children: the sun is gone down
And the dews of night arise.
Come, come leave off play and let us away,
Till the morning appears in the skies.'

'No, no let us play, for it is yet day
And we cannot go to sleep.
Besides, in the sky the little birds fly,
And the hills are all covered with sheep.'

'Well, well go and play till the light fades away,
And then go home to bed.'
The little ones leaped and shouted and laughed
And all the hills echoed.

The same question that was used for the poem by Pope can apply again here:

How do the form and language of this poem contribute to its effect on the reader?

It can be broken down into the following shorter questions:

1. What is the genre of this poem and how do you know? **(Genre)**
2. What use does Blake make of sound patterns in this poem? **(Shapes and patterns)**
3. What words in the poem refer to sounds made? *(Shapes and patterns)*
4. What words are repeated in the poem? **(Shapes and patterns)**
5. What voices are heard in the poem? **(Narrative/Voices in Texts)**
6. What words and ideas are contrasted in the poem? **(Creativity)**
7. What do your answers to these questions tell you about the poem's possible meaning?

Suggestions for Answer

1. The poem's title identifies the poem as a *song*, and gives some sort of identity to the voice that is 'singing' the song – *nurse*. This title also identifies the **genre** of the poem; it tells the reader what sort of text it is.
2. As readers we have certain expectations of songs, including that there will clearly be 'musical' effects within the language. There is a very strong sense of rhyme in this poem, created sometimes by monosyllabic rhymes; these occur both at the end of lines ('hill'/'still') and within lines ('sky'/'fly'). There are also, though, less strong rhymes or half-rhymes. These are found, for example, in the first lines of stanzas one and two – 'children'/'green' and 'children'/ 'down'. This mixture of strong rhymes and less obvious echoes of rhymes contributes to the wider effect of the poem's very strong rhythm, with many of the syllables being stressed.

    The last stanza has some subtle differences in the way its sounds come across. The third line, unlike all the other stanzas, has only a half-rhyme between 'leaped' and 'laughed'. The second line sets up the expectation of a very strong rhyming finish with the single syllable and stressed word 'bed'. Instead, though, there is the much more unexpected 'echoed'. If said with a modern two syllable stress, then the word falls very flat; if with a three syllable stress (ech/o/ed) then the word itself becomes iconic, in that it actually sounds like what it means. Instead of there being a finality to the poem, which there would have been with a strong rhyme, the children's laughter continues to reverberate and bounce back, so having even more value.
3. This poem announces in its title that it is a 'song' – in other words it is proclaiming that it has sound qualities, as we have seen above. The poem also, however, contains words that denote sound – 'voices', 'heard', 'laughing', 'shouted', 'laughed', 'echoed' – and the absence of sound in 'still'. Clearly making a noise and being heard are important to the poem's overall meanings.
4. As you would expect with a song, there are numerous repetitions of words. Often these repetitions are adjacent to each other: 'Come', 'come'; 'No', 'no'; 'Well', 'well'. Other repetitions include 'all', 'hill'/'hills', 'play', 'sky'/'skies', 'children', 'little' and 'laughing'/'laughed'. The idea of laughing, appearing as it does both

near the beginning and end of the poem, is clearly significant, suggesting innocent happiness. The word 'echoed' also involves the idea of repetition in its meaning. The hills are bouncing back the sounds of the children.

One word, though, appears ten times within the four verses of the poem. 'And' might on the surface of appear to be an unimportant word, but not when it is used this often. It is used at the beginning of a line, and so in a sense foregrounded, seven times, and sometimes in this position it is also stressed. The word 'and' contributes significantly to the apparent simplicity of the poem – using the connective 'and' is often seen as a childish thing to do. In a broader sense it also highlights the fact that we should not necessarily ignore the effect of the apparently less significant words when looking at texts.

5. Although we are told that this is 'the' or 'a' nurse's song, there are at least two 'voices' in the poem, possibly three. One sees the nurse urging care and caution; the other belongs to the children wanting carefree freedom. These voices are set in some sort of opposition to each other, with the children winning the argument. It is their laughter we hear at the end of the poem. If the narrator of the first verse is seen as different from the nurse, and that is possible, then there are three voices, and three viewpoints. If there is a third **narrative voice** in the poem, then it comes right at the start, and it establishes a strong point of view. If the nurse narrates the first verse, it is an opinion. If it is a narrative persona whose voice is heard in the first verse, it is a voice with authority.

6. Although the poem has no obvious metaphor, there is contrast in the poem between day/light and dark/night, which have potentially symbolic values. Traditionally we associate the light with positive aspects and the dark with negative. The cautious nurse wants the children home before dark sets in, before danger comes, but the children want to play longer, to take full advantage of the light, even if that might involve the risk of staying out too long.

7. We have noted above that the poem has very little obvious metaphor, as we would expect, having identified its simplicity of approach. It could be, though, that the whole poem is a metaphor, that children's voices being heard and the hills responding is a celebration of innocence. The experience of the nurse urges caution, but the exuberance of the innocent triumphs. Students who have studied any Blake will know that Blake wrote poems under the headings of *Innocence* and *Experience* and that these notions of adult responsibility and childhood innocence are major themes in his work.

It was noted earlier that analysing the language of literature serves little purpose if it is done in a vacuum, and that you should not isolate the language from everything else that is going on. Meanings and language work together, not separately.

The analysis of the poem above has looked at a number of structural aspects, and has commented on repetition and what it contributes to the poem. It has also implied that this very 'traditional' poem – traditional in the sense of its regular form, rhyme and so on – is in fact far subtler than it seems. If a range of meanings can be found in the poem, then, paradoxically, the poem's very simplicity will have contributed to its effect.

The meanings that have been hinted at in the analysis so far concern two opposing sets of voices which form a sort of debate. On the one hand are the children asking for 'play', and on the other the nurse who seems concerned for their safety. Childhood innocence is set against adult experience but not in an aggressive sense. The children ask for permission and the permission is granted. The third voice, which could be a narrative persona, or the nurse, or Blake himself, endorses at the start of the poem what happens at the end of the it; children's voices/laughter produce rest and stillness in those who hear them. The **passive voice** when used in 'are heard' and 'is heard' could suggest that this third voice does not actually hear the voices; it just knows that others do – in which case it could even be the voice of God we are given at the start of the poem.

This idea of a religious dimension to the poem is endorsed by a number of words and ideas in the poem – light and dark, stillness, nature and so on. These do not have to be taken as religious, but they can be, especially when this poem is put in the context of other poems by Blake. Students studying Blake's poetry as a set text would know that he has a reputation as a mystic poet, and would know other works by him which contain similar possibilities. But even those seeing this poem for the first time could look closely at the language and form of the poem and see that it has several potential meanings.

Exercise 3

William Blake wrote two parallel poems called 'Nurse's Song'. The poem from *Songs of Innocence* has been analysed above. As an extension exercise to work on the ideas introduced in this chapter, the other poem, taken from *Songs of Experience* will prove a useful contrast. It is likely that your study of poetry at AS/A2 will involve looking at a collection/selection of poems, so writing comparatively about texts, rather than about texts in isolation, is a skill you need to develop.

Suggestions for answer can be found at the back of the book.

Task: *How do the form and language of this poem compare to the other* 'Nurse's Song'?

Nurse's Song (Experience)

When the voices of children are heard on the green
And whisp'rings are in the dale,
The days of my youth rise fresh in my mind:
My face turns green and pale.

Then come home my children, the sun is gone down
And the dews of night arise;
Your spring and your day are wasted in play,
And your winter and night in disguise.

SUMMARY

This chapter has done the following:

- Indicated some of the ways in which examination questions require the analysis of literary language
- Given an outline of different aspects of literary language
- Introduced some of the main ideas in this book by exploring a short poem by Pope, plus two poems by Blake

STRUCTURE: SHAPES AND PATTERNS

Although, in one sense, literature is created through the use of words, it is not enough to analyse literary texts at the level of words only. After all, there are not many instances where single words have stand-alone meaning. 'Hello', 'goodbye' are a couple of possible examples, but even these do not mean much without a more specific context; we need more than words to create meanings. In this chapter you will be shown how to identify the various ways in which texts have shape and patterns which contribute to their overall meanings

In this chapter and those which follow, the word 'structure' will be used to describe the processes by which texts are built. In using the phrase 'the way texts are built' there are two metaphors at work, and they have a lot in common. The word 'text' comes from the whole notion of textiles, in other words of weaving together. A written text is something that a writer has woven together: a written text is something for you to unpick in your analysis. (This idea of text has many other common uses: we lose the thread, we unravel meanings, readers/authors tie up the loose ends, we look at the material.)

The second metaphor, which, like the idea of text has become so embedded in our language that we barely recognise it as a metaphor at all is the idea that texts have been built, that they are structures. In a very literal sense to say that texts have structure is to use a mixed metaphor, because it is using ideas of weaving and building at the same time, but because the metaphorical origins have faded, we don't really notice. Instead we are more likely to see that weaving and building have in common the idea that something is not only created, but that it is created to a design. The fabric may be colourful, the building may be ornate, but however distinctive they look, they have been created in an organised way.

So, if we pursue the metaphor of building further, we can say that a building has external features such as overall shape and design which indicate what sort of building it is, and what purpose we expect it to fulfil. A school, for example, will be recognisable from the outside, partly because of the way it advertises itself and partly because it will have recognisable external features. Go inside the school and its internal features such as classrooms and offices will confirm the impression. In the same way, literary texts have some aspects to do with the whole text, what it looks like from the outside, and other aspects to do with the way the separate parts hold together, what it looks like from the inside.

SHAPES AND PATTERNS IN POETRY

Exercise 1

To explore these ideas further, and to see some of the ideas which come under the heading of structure in poetry, we will initially look at a poem by Oliver Goldsmith.

> **An Elegy on the Death of a Mad Dog**
>
> Good people all, of every sort,
> Give ear unto my song;
> And if you find it wond'rous short
> It cannot hold you long.
>
> In Islington there was a man,
> Of whom the world might say
> That still a godly race he ran,
> Whene'er he went to pray.
>
> A kind and gentle heart he had,
> To comfort friends and foes;
> The naked every day he clad,
> When he put on his clothes.
>
> And in that town a dog was found,
> As many dogs there be,
> Both mongrel, puppy, whelp and hound
> And curs of low degree.
>
> This man and dog at first were friends;
> But when a pique began,
> The dog, to gain some private ends,
> Went mad and bit the man.
> Around from all the neighbouring
> streets
> The wondering neighbours ran,
> And swore the dog had lost its wits,
> To bite so good a man.
>
> The wound it seemed both sore and sad
> To every Christian eye;
> And while they swore the dog was mad,
> They swore the man would die.
>
> But soon a wonder came to light,
> That showed the rogues they lied:
> The man recovered of the bite,
> The dog it was that died.
>
> Oliver Goldsmith (1766)

Having read the poem carefully answer the following questions:

1. Each stanza of this poem contributes to its growing plot. Write a brief paragraph on what each stanza offers to the development of the story that it tells.
2. What use of sound patterns, such as rhyme and rhythm, can be found in the poem?
3. What other forms of repetition are in the poem?
4. What grammatical patterns can you find in the poem?
5. What point is made at the end of the poem?

Suggestions for Answer

This poem, despite calling itself an elegy, is not really an elegy at all. It is instead a poem with a moral, saying that we should not be deceived by appearances. There are many people who seem pious and god-fearing on the outside, but the reality is that they use religion to hide their true selves.

Because this poem has a moral, and is therefore a sort of fable, it tells a story to make its point. The poem has a plot line, and each stanza of the poem adds an element to this. So the poem begins with an order that 'good people' should heed what is to follow, and it ends with the death of the dog. The moral, therefore, is not explicitly pointed out: it is left to the reader to work out the real point of the story. The story is told in strict chronological order. After the injunction of stanza 1, stanzas 2 and 3 describe the man. Stanza 4 describes the dog. Stanza 5 moves the story forward quickly, establishing friendship between man and dog before the dog bites the man. Stanzas 6 and 7 show public reaction to this event, and their expectation of what will happen next. The final stanza reverses this expectation.

A significant part of the poem's structure is its use of sound patterns. In particular Goldsmith uses rhyme and rhythm in a very consistent way. So each stanza has alternate lines which rhyme, and many of these rhymes are full rhymes, such as 'song'/'long'. Goldsmith varies the type of rhyme occasionally, however. Full rhymes can be restricting to a poet in their choice of words and can become very monotonous in their effect. So in addition to the full rhymes there are half-rhymes. There are vowel rhymes in 'foes'/'clothes', 'be'/'degree' and 'began'/'man', called vowel rhymes because it is the vowel sounds that are repeated. There is also a consonant rhyme with 'streets'/'wits' where the 't's are repeated. As you would expect, though, the final rhyme is a full rhyme, giving the poem a very definite conclusion.

The rhythm of the poem, helped of course by the rhyme, is strong and insistent. In the first two lines, for example, it can be argued that, of the thirteen syllables, ten are stressed. This heavy stress pattern is what we would expect of a poem which calls itself a 'song', and is enhanced by the deliberate omission of some syllables as in 'wond'rous' and 'whene'er'.

As well as repeated sounds, there are also repeated words. The two most obviously repeated are 'dog'/'dogs' (8 times) and 'man' (6 times). It is not just their repetition that is important, though – it is the fact that they are used unchangingly to refer to the two main characters in the story. Usually both men and dogs have names, but not here. This refusal to give them identities helps with the idea that this is a moral fable rather than a 'real' story. The man in particular stands for a type of man rather than an individual. Other important words which are repeated include 'swore', 'mad' and 'die'/'died'.

Repetition in vocabulary can go beyond the identical use of the same word. Where words and phrases are in the same area of meaning, they are said to exist in the same **semantic field**. Here, then, we have group of words to describe the apparently virtuous: there are 'good people', 'a godly race he ran', 'so good a man' and 'every Christian eye', although in the final stanza such people have become 'rogues'. Contrast, by reference to something else that has gone before, is also a sort of repetition. This is especially noticeable in the final stanza, where there is a contrast between what is expected (the man will die) and what actually happens (the dog dies).

Another aspect of repetition/patterning that should always be considered is the grammatical structures that are used, especially where they have significant impact on the text and reader by drawing attention to themselves. One obvious aspect of **grammar** in this poem involves word order. Poets in particular are likely to alter the usual word order in order to help with rhythm and rhyme. So, in stanza 2 Goldsmith places 'In Islington' before 'there was a man'; try saying it in reverse order and the rhythm is broken. Stanza 4 contains the same structure in its first line, as arguably does stanza 6. The opening line of the seventh stanza has an added 'it' to its structure.

By the time we reach the last line of the poem, then, we are already used to some unusual word orders. It is in the last line that this happens to the most significant effect, however. As it is the last line, and it completes a rhyme, there is an expectation that there will be a final impact, that the poem will make its point. This impact is largely due to the inversion of the word order – instead of 'it was the dog that died' we get 'The dog it was . . .' This means that all the weight of the rhythm goes on 'dog', allowing surprise to be registered by the weight of emphasis. They all thought it would be the man killed by infection, but it was the dog who picked up the poison from the man.

SHAPES AND PATTERNS IN NOVELS

It is usually seen to be much easier to talk about the structure of a poem than it is about the structure of a novel or a play. To continue the metaphor of buildings, most poems are small houses, while novels in particular are like huge university campuses. The only way to get a sense of the whole thing is by boarding an aircraft and taking an aerial photograph. It can be difficult to get a complete picture.

One method for thinking about the way novels are structured is to make use of their component parts.

So you can consider how:

- Chapters relate to each other and to the novel as a whole
- Paragraphing relates to the chapter
- Sentences relate to the paragraph
- Words and phrases relate to sentences

This model gives you some sense of things to look for, but, as it stands, it fails to take account of some overall **discourse** features which govern the organisation of a novel. The word 'discourse' has various meanings in English studies, but here it is used to refer to organising factors which give a text its overall **cohesion**. Discourse features, therefore, will include structural aspects such as narrative point of view, chronology and genre. These are such significant aspects of the way literary texts work that they are discussed at length in other chapters in this book. In doing this, though, it is not being suggested that they operate separately in texts.

Another way in which discourse works in texts is in the ideas and ideologies which lie behind the novel. Put in simple terms, Charles Dickens's dislike of child poverty is as much an organising principle of *Oliver Twist* as the way he organises his narrative or arranges his chapters. In this book, which is not concerned with specific texts, this area of discourse cannot really be explored, but you should always remember that structural aspects of texts do not exist in isolation: they give shape and expression to the plots and ideas which the author wants to present to the reader.

Exercise 2

The following extract is the first three paragraphs of Chapter 5 of Mary Shelley's novel *Frankenstein*. In this chapter Frankenstein 'gives birth' to the creature. It is a scene made famous by many film versions, both serious and spoofs, and so to some extent the modern reader has expectations of this scene which turn out to be misleading.

A typical exam question to go with this extract would be something like:

Examine the ways in which Shelley presents the horror of the creation in this extract.

To help you disentangle some of the potential elements of this question, read the passage twice. On the second reading make notes on the following:

1. What does each of the three paragraphs deal with in terms of general content?
2. What treatment of time can you find here?
3. What features of sentence structure do you notice here?
4. What groupings can you make in terms of the words used?

Frankenstein, Chapter 5

It was on a dreary night of November that I beheld the accomplishment of my toils. With an anxiety that almost amounted to agony, I collected the instruments of life around me, that I might infuse a spark of being into the lifeless thing that lay at my feet. It was already one in the morning; the rain pattered dismally against the panes, and my candle was nearly burnt out, when, by the glimmer of the half-extinguished light, I saw the dull yellow eye of the creature open; it breathed hard, and a convulsive motion agitated its limbs.

How can I describe my emotions at this catastrophe, or how delineate the wretch whom with such infinite pains and care I had endeavoured to form? His limbs were in proportion, and I had selected his features as beautiful. Beautiful! Great God! His yellow skin scarcely covered the work of muscles and arteries beneath; his hair was of a lustrous black, and flowing; his teeth of pearly whiteness; but these luxuriances only formed a more horrid contrast with his watery eyes, that seemed almost of the same colour as the dun-white sockets in which they were set, his shrivelled complexion and straight black lips.

The different accidents of life are not so changeable as the feelings of human nature. I had worked hard for nearly two years, for the sole purpose of infusing life into an inanimate body. For this I had deprived myself of rest and health. I had desired it with an ardour that far exceeded moderation; but now that I had finished, the beauty of the dream vanished, and breathless horror and disgust filled my heart. Unable to endure the aspect of the being I had created, I rushed out of the room and continued a long time traversing my bedchamber, unable to compose my mind to sleep. At length lassitude succeeded to the tumult I had before endured, and I threw myself on the bed in my clothes, endeavouring to seek a few moments of forgetfulness. But it was in vain: I slept, indeed, but I was disturbed by the wildest dreams. I thought I saw Elizabeth, in the bloom of health, walking in the streets of Ingolstadt. Delighted and surprised, I embraced her, but as I imprinted the first kiss on her lips, they became livid with the hue of death; her features appeared to change, and I thought that I held the corpse of my dead mother in my arms; a shroud enveloped her form, and I saw the grave-worms crawling in the folds of the flannel. I started from my sleep with horror; a cold dew covered my forehead, my teeth chattered, and every limb became convulsed; when, by the dim and yellow light of the moon, as it forced its way through the window shutters, I beheld the wretch – the miserable monster whom I had created. He held up the curtain of the bed; and his eyes, if eyes they may be called, were fixed on me. His jaws opened, and he muttered some inarticulate sounds, while a grin wrinkled his cheeks. He might have spoken, but I did not hear, one hand was stretched out, seemingly to detain me, but I escaped and rushed downstairs. I took refuge in the courtyard belonging to the house which I inhabited, where I remained during the rest of the night, walking up and down in the greatest agitation, listening attentively, catching and fearing each sound as if it were to announce the approach of the daemoniacal corpse to which I had so miserably given life.

Suggestions for Answer

If you were studying this novel as a set text, you would know it well enough to comment on its **narrative voice**, which in this case belongs to Frankenstein, and aspects of the Gothic genre. Here, though, we will look at this extract in terms of time/place, syntax and vocabulary.

There are a number of ways of looking at these three paragraphs as structural units. One obvious feature is the sheer length of the paragraphs. The third in particular contains a vast amount of content, much more than would typically be found in a modern novel. Despite the frantic action and emotion that are being described, the paragraphing seems to the modern reader to be rather cumbersome.

The first paragraph both sets the scene in terms of time and place and describes the moment of the creature's 'birth'. The second paragraph describes Frankenstein's emotional response to what he has made and then describes the creature itself. The third paragraph shows Frankenstein reflecting on the past, before reacting in the present: he leaves the room; he sleeps and dreams; he wakes to find the creature looking at him; he rushes out again and takes refuge for the rest of the night.

Because novels tell stories, time is always likely to be a structural feature. Here, Shelley chooses a November night, November being a month associated with damp and gloom, night also being associated with darkness. At the very moment of the creature's birth, though, we are taken back over the two years of work that have gone into the grisly project before returning again to a sequence of events which follow each other as the night progresses.

If we now look at the second paragraph, it allows us to see an example of the way sentences contribute to the paragraph as a whole. Another word for the structure of sentences is **syntax**, and here there are a number of significant variations, variations which contribute to the overall effect of what is being described. So, the paragraph begins with two **rhetorical questions**, questions which imply an answer rather than expect one. Both of these are in a way answered. The reader can work out the horror that must be felt, by the description of the creature which is indeed 'delineated' for us. The straightforward **compound sentence** beginning 'His limbs were in proportion' is followed by two exclamations. When the description is given, though, it is contained in one long, **complex sentence** which is itself subdivided by the use of the semi-colon.

If we use the third paragraph to explore its vocabulary, we can see lots of examples of words being in the same areas of meaning – the same semantic field. These words can be grouped not only according to their meaning but also through their grammatical function. So, for example, if we look for verbs describing physical movement we find among others 'rushed', 'threw', 'started', 'chattered', 'forced', – all suggesting violent physical movement, a sense of urgency and panic. By contrast, the creature is much more still, with its eyes 'fixed' and its hand 'stretched'.

Another semantic field involves the nouns and noun phrases that describe the monster: it is 'the wretch', 'the miserable monster', 'the daemoniacal corpse'. In terms of contrast, though, note that throughout the extract the creature is sometimes 'it' and sometimes 'he' – the creature, by the inconsistent use of these pronouns hovers between being human and not human. These are only two of many clusters of words in this long paragraph. Look also for words of horror and repulsion, peace and tumult.

STRUCTURE IN DRAMA

Although the word 'drama' can refer to stage plays, radio plays, television plays and so forth, the reality of English Literature courses at AS/A2 is that stage plays are the most frequently studied. Of the three types of text you have to study – poetry, novels, plays – a play is the least 'readerly' form. Although it can be read by an individual, it is best seen and heard in performance, in a production made either for stage or film. In English courses you are, if writing about plays in exams, *writing about your reading of a work that was written to be seen and heard*. This means you need to show some sophisticated understanding if you are to analyse how a play works.

Drama, especially stage drama, cannot be approached in the way you approach novels. However many readings you may be able to make of a novel or a poem, the text in front of you is always there. With a stage play, though, you have to consider another layer – that only in a performance does the play come into existence, and it is usually watched without any written text at all. So you, as a student, have a script before you which is a sort of halfway house between the playwright writing and the actors performing.

A play tells its story through speech and actions. Stage drama is limited in what it can show; unlike film or radio drama it cannot range widely in a geographical sense. Time is another issue which playwrights must consider. They cannot show everything that happens in the story, because, unlike a novel, there is a relatively fixed amount of time available. This limitation of time means that characters must also be established quickly. Playwrights have to use certain techniques to suggest space, time, character and events before and beyond those that are to be physically shown, and you as a student have to understand that this is being done so that the play can work on stage.

The word **dramatisation** refers to the way writers construct and shape their plays (rather than what the play is about in terms of theme/plot). Some aspects of the structure of plays to look out for are as follows:

1. **Act and scene divisions:** These help you to consider aspects of time, not only time that is seen, but time that is referred to as already having passed. In most plays characters have to talk about the past as well as the present. They also have to report actions that have taken place, but for various reasons cannot be shown on stage. In some plays, notably those by Shakespeare, the act divisions are rarely noticed in performance, but the scene changes are often signalled by the use of rhyming couplets. In other plays a division is made by blackouts, the playing of music, intervals, scene shifting and other techniques.

2. **Stage Directions:** Tennessee Williams sets the following scene at the beginning of *A Streetcar Named Desire*:

   It is first dark of an early evening in May. The sky that shows around the dim white building is a peculiarly tender blue . . .

   Williams gives information here that cannot fully be perceived by an audience. How would they know it's May? Or that the blue is meant to be tender? Williams is writing like a novelist here, setting the scene, establishing a verbal sense of time and place that the technicians will try in part to achieve. Many playwrights use stage directions to give a broad sense of what they are trying to achieve. Although these directions are not part of the spoken play as performed, they can be very helpful to students as readers of a play.

3. **Who is on stage and who is not:** Characters in plays can be on stage or off, and they can make entrances and exits – these factors are always significant in the way a play unfolds. If a character is off stage, and so does not hear what other characters and the audience hear, then there is considerable potential for humour, intrigue or both.

   In some plays characters talk aloud to 'themselves', with the audience overhearing, or they even address the audience directly. This use of **soliloquy** is explored further in Chapter 5.

4. **Who hears conversation and who does not:** One technique that is sometimes used by playwrights to structure their plays is to use eavesdropping or overhearing. Although audiences are happy to accept the idea of eavesdropping

in plays, it rarely happens in real spoken situations. When a play contains examples of eavesdropping, they only work if the audience knows what is going on, and at least one of the characters does not. This means that we, the audience, must see the eavesdropper. The effects of this can vary; it can be a form of spying and so lead to intrigue, or it can lead to mistakes and so be comic.

5. **What does the audience know and when does it find out:** In real-life talk, conversation involves **pragmatics**, that is, a shared understanding of the context of what is being said. Most talk involves only those who are taking part, so no consideration needs to be given to outsiders. Talk in plays, though, has to be clear to the audience, and so is much more transparent: characters not only talk to each other; they talk in front of an audience in such a way that the audience understands the significance of what is being said.

   This does not mean, though, that the audience knows everything they need to right at the start. A playwright will often release information slowly, especially if the play involves some sort of mystery. By the end of the play, though, the audience will usually know all there is to know within the world of the play.

6. **Who takes part in conversation and who does not:** The time a character is on stage will be divided between times that they talk and times that they do not talk – unless they are delivering a soliloquy (see above). Characters not talking can be as significant as when they are talking, especially if they are drawing attention to themselves in some non-verbal way.

7 **Where the action is taking place:** Stage drama is much more limited in its locations than film or television drama. This means that shown locations are usually important, while shifting these locations signals something significant. Sometimes, for example in Shakespeare's plays, the locations are identified verbally rather than visually. So *Hamlet* begins, we are told by the stage notes at *Elsinore. A platform before the castle.* This is not seen by the audience, though – they find out from what is said that guards are on watch outside a Danish castle.

8. **The management of time:** A crucial aspect of a play's structure involves the way time 'works'. The time it takes to perform a play is usually about two to three hours, usually with an interval or two included. The timescale of the play's action is usually much longer than this, though, often spanning years of time. How playwrights manage this 'problem' is a crucial factor in the way they structure their works. Although in the written text version they can write 'two years later', they also need to build this into the action and dialogue so that an audience can detect it.

Exercise 3

This section on dramatisation has focused on aspects of drama which are particular to stage plays. Using the sections above, make notes on some of the structural aspects of a stage play that you are studying.

Exercise 4

Plays when read as texts by you alone – a difficult process – will usually take even less time to read than they take to perform. This is because in performance there are visual, physical and line delivery issues which a solo reading cannot give. To explore further the issues around studying play texts on English courses, look at the following extract which is the opening of Steven Berkoff's play *West*. It is set in Stamford Hill, London. Then look, if possible, at the opening two scenes of Shakespeare's *Hamlet*.

What issues are raised for you as a reader of the text below which you would need to show awareness of when writing about the play?

Some suggestions for answer are at the back of the book.

West

Pub sequence. All begin to sing as the lights go up.

RALPH: 'My old man . . .'
MIKE: 'I'm forever blowing bubbles . . .'
KEN: 'Roll out the barrel . . .'
SYLV: 'You are my sunshine . . .'
    (Les and others join sing-song)
SID: Time, gentlemen, please. Your glasses . . .
    (All speak in turn: 'Night, Sylv', 'Night, all', 'Ring me', 'See ya', etc. etc.)
SID   (*To Pearl*): Feel any happier?
PEARL: Well, it makes a change anyway.
    (They exit from the pub, leaving boys and Sylv. The GANG explodes on the stage and freezes.)
LES: Breathless, I was aghast when I saw/standing between the full moon and the blinking lamplight, this geezer/all armed, a certain aim he took/and felled the swarthy git from Hoxton with a deft and subtle chop/I never witnessed Mike I swear such venom and gross form in leather stacked/his coat stitched and embellished with fine lattice work of studs (to be more deadly when swung) no other weapon being handy like.
MIKE: Armed you say?
RALPH: From top to toe.
STEVE: From head to foot.
MIKE: Then saw you not his face?
KEN: He wore his titfer up.
MIKE: By Christ, would I had been there.
LES: He would have much amazed you.

SUMMARY

This chapter has done the following:

- Explored what is meant by terms such as form and structure
- Looked at ways of analysing structure in examples of each of the three major genres – poetry, prose and drama
- Highlighted some of the issues faced when studying a play text that is written to be performed

GENRE

This chapter explores the importance of genre when discussing the language of literature. Genre and language are so intertwined that asking what comes first, the genre or the language, is as pointless as asking the same question of the chicken and the egg. The fact is that language helps to define and shape the genre, while the genre gives the language its shape and purpose. Thinking about genre is useful in many aspects of studying texts, especially when you are asked to compare texts in various ways, and/or when you are being asked to consider different interpretations of texts. Although placing a text in a genre categorises a text, these categories are never fixed.

GENRE AND SUBGENRE

Rather confusingly, the word 'genre' has a number of different applications within the study of literary texts. On the one hand it refers to very broad definitions of types of text: poetry, prose and drama. On the other, 'genre' refers to much more specific categories of texts such as sonnets or crime fiction. But because crime fiction is itself too vague a term for some of the specialised types of crime fiction, **subgenres** are constantly being formed: these include police procedural, forensic, lesbian detective, court procedural and so on.

Who is it, though, who create these genres, who suggest that texts be linked together through category? In short, all those who have a vested interest in the text: authors often see themselves working within genres, readers identify a product that they know they like and which lives up to certain expectations, and publishers can build up their sales by trading on what they know is commercially successful.

DIFFERENCE AND SIMILARITY

The two key factors which determine the way we categorise texts are *difference* and *similarity*. If one text differs from another, then they do not belong in a certain category. If, on the other hand, they are similar, then they can be put in another category. This all means that 'genre' is used not only to describe broad types of literary texts; it is also used in a much more specific sense. All of the following can be seen as similarities through which genres are created: *of acceptation*

- Similarity of *formal* arrangement (i.e. a sonnet)
- Similarity of *content* (i.e. crime, science fiction)
- Similarity of *narrative method* (i.e. first person unreliable narrative)
- Similarity of *intended audience* (i.e. designed for a specific age group)
- Similarity of *intended response* (i.e. tragedy to make you think, comedy to make you laugh)
- Similarity of *occasion* (i.e. written for weddings or funerals)
- Similarity of *time* (i.e. belonging to the same period of time when written)
- Similarity of *production* (i.e. made by the same group of people, although they may not think of themselves as a group at the time)
- Similarity of *authorship* (i.e. Shakespeare standing alone: we study 'Shakespeare')

Exercise 1

All of the categories of genre above will, at least in part, determine the way language is used and at the same time be determined by the way language is used. As a brief opening exercise look again at the two poems below which have been seen in previous chapters.

Put these two poems in various genres. Suggestions for answer follow.

Epigram from the French

Sir, I admit your gen'ral rule
That every poet is a fool:
But you yourself may serve to show it,
That every fool is not a poet.
Alexander Pope (1732)

An Elegy on the Death of a Mad Dog

Good people all, of every sort,
Give ear unto my song;
And if you find it wond'rous short
It cannot hold you long.

In Islington there was a man,
Of whom the world might say
That still a godly race he ran,
Whene'er he went to pray.

A kind and gentle heart he had,
To comfort friends and foes;
The naked every day he clad,
When he put on his clothes.

And in that town a dog was found,
As many dogs there be,
Both mongrel, puppy, whelp and hound
And curs of low degree.

This man and dog at first were friends;
But when a pique began,
The dog, to gain some private ends,
Went mad and bit the man.

Around from all the neighbouring streets
The wondering neighbours ran,
And swore the dog had lost its wits,
To bite so good a man.

The wound it seemed both sore and sad
To every Christian eye;
And while they swore the dog was mad,
They swore the man would die.

But soon a wonder came to light,
That showed the rogues they lied:
The man recovered of the bite,
The dog it was that died.

Oliver Goldsmith (1766)

Suggestions for Answer

In an exercise such as this, the answers given really are suggestions, because there is no fixed number of right answers. Here are some possibilities:

- Both are poems
- Both are rhyming poems
- Both are written by men
- Both are written in the same century
- Both are satirical in the points they make
- Both refer to their genre in their titles

Looking at the full list, it should be clear that saying both are poems is not a particularly helpful category to put them in – it is too broad. On the other hand saying that both refer to their genre in their titles is much more specific. We can then add to this statement a contrast: both refer to their genre in their titles, but the second poem is not really an elegy at all. What we are now showing is the similarity yet difference which is the hallmark of genre.

Exercise 2

Most of the rest of this chapter will involve a longer exercise looking at literary texts and thinking about how they can be categorised.

Read the extracts from texts which follow. Then consider the different ways in which various pairs (or more) of texts can be put in a category together and if possible some differences between the texts in that category too. Some suggestions for answers are at the back of the book.

1. Extract from *Bridget Jones Diary* by Helen Fielding

Noon. London: my flat. Ugh. The last thing on earth I feel physically, emotionally or mentally equipped to do is drive to Una and Geoffrey Alconbury's New Year's Day Turkey Curry Buffet in Grafton Underwood. Geoffrey and Una Alconbury are my parents' best friends and, as Uncle Geoffrey never tires of reminding me, have known me since I was running round the lawn with no clothes on. My mother rang up at 8:30 in the morning last August Bank Holiday and forced me to promise to go. She approached it via a cunningly circuitous route.

'Oh, hello, darling. I was just ringing to see what you wanted for Christmas.'
'Christmas?'
'Would you like a surprise, darling?'
'No!' I bellowed. 'Sorry. I mean . . .'
'I wondered if you'd like a set of wheels for your suitcase.'
'But I haven't got a suitcase.'

2. Extract from *Gulliver's Travels* by Jonathan Swift (1724)

The Emperor lays on the table three fine silken threads of six inches long. One is blue, the other red, and the third green. These threads are proposed as prizes for those persons whom the Emperor has a mind to distinguish by a peculiar mark of his favour. The ceremony is performed in his Majesty's great chamber of state, where the candidates are to undergo a trial of dexterity very different from the former, and such as I have not observed the least resemblance of in any other country of the old or the new world. The Emperor holds a stick in his hands, both ends parallel to the horizon, while the candidates, advancing one by one, sometimes leap over the stick, sometimes creep under it backwards and forwards several times, according as the stick is advanced or depressed. Sometimes the Emperor holds one end of the stick, and his first minister the other; sometimes the minister has it entirely to himself. Whoever performs his part with most agility, and holds out the longest in leaping and creeping, is rewarded with the blue-coloured silk; the red is given to the next, and the green to the third, which they all wear girt twice round about the middle; and you see few great persons about this court who are not adorned with one of these girdles.

3. Extract from *Samuel Pepys's Diary*

September 2, 1666

Some of our maids, sitting up late last night to get things ready against our feast day today, Jane called us up about three in the morning, to tell us of a great fire they saw in the city. So I rose and slipped on my nightgown and went to her window, and thought it to be on the backside of Marke-Lane at the farthest; but being unused to such fires as followed, I thought it far enough off; and so went to bed again and to sleep . . . By and by Jane comes and tells me that above 300 houses have been burned down tonight by the fire we saw, and that it is now burning down all Fish-street by London Bridge.

4. Extract from *Paradise Lost*, Book IX,
by John Milton (1674)

(At this point in the poem, Eve eats the forbidden fruit)

> So saying, her rash hand in evil hour
> Forth reaching to the fruit, she pluckd, she eat:
> Earth felt the wound, and Nature from her seat
> Sighing through all her Works gave signs of woe,
> That all was lost.

5. A text message poem

Can u c me

cos i can c u lk lft lk right im in
sght im 1 of da crowd dat lies
b4 yr eyes bt can u tel whch
face is mine an bsides all dat
wld u lik wot u'd find?

(*Guardian*, 5 April 2001)

6. Extract from *Notes from a Small Island* by Bill Bryson

I was heading for Newcastle by way of York when I did another impetuous thing. I got off at Durham, intending to poke around the cathedral for an hour or so and fell in love with it instantly in a serious way. Why, it's wonderful – a perfect little city – and I kept thinking: 'Why did no-one tell me about this?' I knew, of course, that it had a fine Norman cathedral but I had no idea that it was so *splendid*. I couldn't believe that not once in twenty years had anyone said to me, 'You've never been to Durham? Good God man, you must go at once! Please take my car.' . . . So let me say it now: if you have never been to Durham, go at once. Take my car. It's wonderful.

7. Extract from *The Rape of the Lock* by Alexander Pope (1714)

(At this point in the poem Belinda, a beautiful young woman has unwillingly had a piece of hair cut off by an admirer)

Then flash'd the living lightning from her eyes,
And screams of horror rend th'affrighted skies.
Nor louder shrieks to pitying heav'n are cast,
When husbands or when lapdogs breathe their last;
Or when rich China vessels fall'n from high,
In glittering dust, and painted fragments lie.

8. *Centaur* by Edwin Morgan

i am, horse
unhorse, me
i am, horse
unhorse, me
i am, horse
unhorse, me
i am, horse
unhorse, me
i am, horse
unhorse, me
i am, horse
unhorse, me
i am, horse
unhorse, me
i am horse:
unhorse me!

(From *Selected Poems*,
Carcanet, 1985)

9. Extract from *King Lear* by William Shakespeare

(This is the opening of Act 1, scene 2 and the first time the audience has seen Edmund)

Enter Edmund reading a letter

EDMUND

Thou, nature, art my goddess; to thy law
My services are bound. Wherefore should I
Stand in the plague of custom, and permit
The curiosity of nations to deprive me,
For that I am some twelve or fourteen moonshines
Lag of a brother? Why bastard? Wherefore base?
When my dimensions are as generous and my shape as true,
As honest madam's issue?

Exercise 3

We have seen in some of the examples above that texts can be placed not only in genres; they can play with notions of genre. Much comedy, visual and written, involves playing with genre conventions and expectations, either making them transparent or mixing them together in unlikely combinations.

The advert on page 31 was in full-page colour in the *Independent on Sunday Review* on 17 May 1998. Write a commentary on the ways in which this advert uses genre to get across its message. Some suggestions for answers appear at the back of the book.

SUMMARY

This chapter has done the following:

- Looked at notions of genre and subgenre, similarity and difference
- Explored issues around the comparison and linking of texts. This reminds us that all texts are in some ways linked to others – no text is purely 'original' in the way that we are sometimes led to believe is the case
- Examined some ideas around the concept of intertextuality. Writers rarely use language in a unique way, they are reshaping language uses that we already know about through our reading of other texts

---

Figure 3.1 Advertisement for a Terry Pratchett Discworld novel, *The Lost Continent*. (*Independent on Sunday Review*, 1998)

NARRATIVE   CHAPTER 4

This chapter will focus on a number of issues which relate to the study of narrative. It will first look at the idea of the narrator and the narratee which appears in many texts including literature. It will then look at first and third person narratives in fiction, which will lead on to an analysis of how much narrators know, and how reliable they are. It will then explore the representation of speech and thought. The chapter closes by looking at chronology in narratives and the reader's point of view.

STORY/PLOT/NARRATIVE

The terms 'story', 'plot' and 'narrative' are sometimes used to refer to much the same thing, but in order to show the importance of narrative, the following distinctions need to be be made:

1. **Story:** the story consists of all the various events which are going to be shown.

2. **Plot:** the plot is the chain of causes and circumstances which connect the various events and place them into some sort of relation with each other.

3. **Narrative:** narrative involves the showing or telling of these events and the various methods used to do this showing. The idea of *knowledge* is useful when we look at the way narrative works. The origin of the words 'narrative', 'narrator' and so on comes from the Greek word *gnarus* which means 'knowing'. A narrator, then, is someone who knows, and the process by which that knowledge is communicated is the narrative.

   Although the word 'narrative' has several possible meanings, it will be used in this chapter to refer to *the process of telling stories*. Whatever English course you are taking, exploring narrative will be an important part of studying texts, especially prose fiction.

   The word 'narrative' is most frequently used in literature courses to describe the process by which novels, short stories and longer poems are relayed to readers. The application of the word 'narrative' is not limited to texts that are usually defined as being literature, though. Many other texts, which normally fall outside the category of literature clearly involve story-telling: consider, for example, a private diary. Although based upon the thoughts and experiences of one person, these experiences are written down and shaped to be read at a later date, even if the writer believes (s)he will be the only person ever to do so. Or consider a piece of travel writing. Although based upon actual experience, this experience is shaped so that it can be presented to others – and it is this *shaping* of the experience which gives the text its narrative.

What has been shown about narrative so far is as follows:

- Many texts, and not just those defined as literary, have a narrative
- Analysing narrative involves looking at aspects of the way a story is told
- Narrative involves knowledge. The narrator knows and tells something that the narratee does not know

TYPES OF NARRATOR: FIRST AND THIRD PERSON

It should already be clear that although a written story has an author, it is not this author who tells the story – it is a narrator created by the author. The most obvious distinction between types of narrator is whether they are third person or first person. A third person will use the pronouns 'he, she, it' or 'they' and a first person narrative will largely use the pronouns 'I' and 'we'.

Examples of each method of narration can be shown using short extracts from Charles Dickens's novel *Bleak House* which has a double narrative, one part in the third person and the other narrated by a young woman, Esther Summerson.

Early in the novel we are given a description of Sir Leicester Deadlock, with the narrative in the third person.

Sir Leicester is twenty years, full measure, older than my Lady. He will never see sixty-five again, nor perhaps sixty-six, nor yet sixty-seven. He has a twist of the gout now and then, and walks a little stiffly. He is of a worthy presence, with his light grey hair and whiskers, his fine shirt-frill, his pure white waistcoat, and his blue coat with bright buttons always buttoned. He is ceremonious, stately, most polite on every occasion to my Lady, and holds her personal attractions in the highest estimation. His gallantry to my Lady, which has never changed since he courted her, is the one little touch of romantic fancy in him.

The first person narrative of Esther Summerson begins:

> I have a great deal of difficulty in beginning to write my portion of these pages, for I know I am not clever. I always knew that. I used to say to my doll, when we were alone together, 'Now Dolly, I am not clever, you know very well, and you must be patient with me, like a dear!'

In the very simplest of terms, we can see the difference established in the narratives by the use of the pronouns 'him'/'his' in the first extract and in the pronoun 'I' in the second. This means that the narrator in the first extract is an observer *outside* the action of the novel, whereas the narrator in the second extract is somehow involved *inside* what is to follow.

Although useful as starting points, though, these distinctions are very general. Further questions need to be asked about the narrators.

HOW MUCH DOES THE NARRATOR KNOW?

We have already noted above that one aspect of narrative involves the idea of knowledge, of how much the narrator knows at any given time. How much knowledge the narrator has needs to be worked out by the reader, although clearly the narrator must know something, or there would be no story to tell at all. Although working out the amount of knowledge shown by the narrator will usually require reading more than a short extract, the examples above from Dickens already give us considerable clues.

Exercise 1

Look again at the two extracts from *Bleak House*:

(a) How much knowledge does the third person narrator have about Sir Leicester Deadlock, and what sort of knowledge is it?
(b) How much knowledge does the first person narrator have and what sort of knowledge is it?

Suggestions for Answer

The third person narrator knows a lot about this man externally, and implies a lot about him as character too. The reader can work out his age, that he has grey hair, how he dresses and so on. We also might guess from the name that he has been given that he is a man set in his ways. We learn that he is stately and polite to his wife, although as readers we may wonder if these are very romantic ways to treat a partner. Our doubts about Sir Leicester are increased by the final sentence. If this is all he can manage in terms of 'romantic fancy', then he is probably a very unimaginative man.

From the evidence of this short extract we can say that the narrator knows quite a bit about this man in terms of his external appearance, which is stated directly, and also about internal aspects of his thought and behaviour, which is implied.

A first person narrative is inevitably limited in its knowledge – by definition a person who is in the action of the story can only know about what they see, do, and are told about, and how they personally react to events. The narrator here does not describe herself in an external way but she does give some clues as to how she sees herself as a person. In other words her knowledge, as shown here, is internal rather than external.

Because the narrator is talking about her own characteristics, rather than about observable detail, we do not have to accept what she says as necessarily 'true'. We may feel that she is too self-critical, and as modern readers we may also find her conversation with her doll horribly sentimental.

Exercise 2

Take a third person story that you know well, such as a fairy tale or fable, and rewrite it using a first person narrative. Consider how the story changes with this new treatment.

HOW RELIABLE IS THE NARRATOR?

A subsidiary question to how much the narrator knows, is how far we can rely on what the narrator tells us. The narrator may apparently have knowledge, knowledge which on closer inspection turns out to be in some way limited.

Exercise 3

Look again at the two extracts from *Bleak House* and assess whether there is a noticeable difference between the two in terms of potential reliability.

Suggestions for Answer

Partly because the narrative is about external detail, we assume that within the world constructed by Dickens the third person narrator can be relied upon to tell the truth. The whole truth will have to emerge gradually, as we cannot expect to know everything at once, but what we are told, we will believe.

The first person narrator, though, seems less reliable. She even tells us to doubt her right at the start, suggesting that she has not the skill to tell her part of the story well. Conversely, though, her very protestations of inadequacy may suggest to the reader that she is honest, that she will do her best to tell the truth. A further issue here involves a question of context: whereas in Dickens's time a typical young woman may have protested her unworthiness and talked to her doll, in modern times we expect our women to be a bit more dynamic. This could mean that while Dickens intends us to have faith in this narrator, as modern readers we are less inclined to do so.

PRESENTING SPEECH

One way in which the narrative can tell us more about a specific character or characters is by the presentation of speech and thought. It is thought in particular which can move the narrative closer to the perspective of one particular character, although it is perfectly possible to give the thoughts of a whole range of characters over the length of a novel. In our everyday lives we cannot know other people's thoughts, but in the worlds of stories we can – to that extent stories give us a unique way of viewing people.

First, though, we will look at speech. As a very broad distinction, speech can be presented in one of two ways – **directly** or **indirectly**. In other words the actual words that a character says can be given to the reader, or they can be reported to the reader by a narrator. This can be seen in the following examples:

Direct Speech

'How can you do this to me?' she asked him forcefully.

Indirect Speech

She asked him forcefully how he could do this to her.

Note that differences in pronouns ('me' becomes 'her'), verbs ('can' becomes 'could') and word order ('can you' / 'he could') distinguish between the two types of speech here.

Direct speech can help with characterisation in particular, because it allows the author to give a character identifiable speech habits. Indirect speech can help to speed up a narrative and avoid the necessity for the more mundane conversations necessary to a plot, which would be dull and time-consuming if endlessly documented.

Another way that speech can be presented to the reader, though, is by using what is known as 'free' speech. This method gives the reader the direct or indirect speech, but not the narrative descriptions that go with it. So, using the example above we would simply be given, usually as part of a longer piece of dialogue:

'How can you do this to me?'
'I don't know what you mean.'

One advantage of this method is that it allows dialogue to move quickly. The reader can usually, with some initial help, identify the speaker by the sequence of the dialogue, but, even so, sometimes readers are forced to backtrack just to check on who is actually saying what.

Direct and indirect speech can be used in both third person and first person narratives, although in first person narratives the only speech that can be given is the speech when the narrator is present.

PRESENTING THOUGHT

The same methods that are used to present speech can also be used to identify characters' thoughts. In narrative terms, what characters think is closer to the 'real' person than what they say, so it is the presentation of thought which can be of particular interest when looking at how writers tell stories. It is the thoughts of characters in particular which move the narrative from an external perspective to a more internal one.

Examples can be shown as follows:

Direct Thought

'How can he do this to me?' she thought.

Indirect Thought

She wondered how he could do this to her.

Note again that differences in pronouns ('me' becomes 'her'), verbs ('can' becomes 'could' and 'thought' becomes 'wondered') and word order ('can he' / 'he could') distinguish between the two types of thought here.

The effect of indirect thought in particular is worth noting at this point. Because no actual thoughts are given, the reported thoughts can be woven seamlessly into the narrative. This means that the narrative can move closer to the perspective of one character without drawing particular attention to the fact.

This effect is even greater when the thought becomes 'free' – in other words a character's thoughts are given, without actually being identified as the character's thoughts. It is as if the character takes over from the narrator for a certain amount of time. Using an expanded version of the example given earlier, the following could appear as free thought:

He grabbed his bag. How could he do this? Then he slammed the door and left.

What happens here is that the narrator, who provides the first and third sentence, hands over to the thoughts of the character in the second sentence without signalling that the handover has taken place. This method of free thought is therefore very flexible, in that it allows the narrative perspective to move freely in and out of the thoughts of different characters. It also means that the reader has to be alert to the subtlety of what is going on.

In Reginald Hill's novel *Dialogues of the Dead*, a young detective named Hat Bowler is working with a superior officer DCI Pascoe. Chapter 12 of the novel, narrated in the third person, begins:

> The good thing about Pascoe was that he didn't nurse grudges, or at least didn't seem to, which might be the bad thing about Pascoe.

At this point in the narrative the reader may presume that this judgement on Pascoe comes from the narrator of the novel. When we read the next paragraph, though, it seems far more likely that we have been given the narrative from Bowler's perspective:

> Hat had volunteered to go and interview Roote about his visit to the Taverna but the DCI had said no, and then, as was usual with him though unusual in most senior officers, gone on to explain his reasoning.

The effect of this is to make us realise that Pascoe does not have definitive characteristics, but characteristics that could be perceived differently by different people – as is the case in the real world we inhabit. This method of narration makes the story less certain in the way it presents people, but arguably more realistic.

Exercise 4

The following extract is taken from Jonathan Coe's novel *The House of Sleep*. Work out the nature of the misunderstanding taking place here and show how Coe creates humour for the reader out of this situation.

In answering this question, consider the following:

- How Coe's presentation of speech here allows the misunderstanding to continue
- Whose thoughts we are given and how are they presented. Look in particular for examples of indirect thought

Suggestions for Answer are at the back of the book.

Sarah nodded. This was not proceeding at all as she had hoped. She wondered how they were possibly going to re-establish the easy, trusting atmosphere of last night's conversation.

'Anyway,' she said, 'I just came to see that you were OK, really. You know, you looked pretty . . . upset last night, and I wanted to know that you were coping.'

'Coping?'

'Well, yes: it must be very hard for you.'

'Oh, you know, it's not such a big deal really. I'll get over it.'

How very male, Sarah thought, to be putting on this bluff display of resilience. Did men really believe that they weren't allowed to show their feelings, even when discussing the death of someone close to them – almost as close, in this case, as it was possible to be? She saw how tense and anxious he was in her presence, how uncomfortable at the thought of having this husk of insensibility peeled back, revealing the softer, truer nature underneath. But she knew that it was in both their interests to persist.

'When I said I thought you'd gone away,' she went on, ' I meant that, you know, the funeral must be soon.'

'Funeral?' said Robert.

'For – I'm sorry, I've forgotten her name . . .'

'For Muriel you mean?'

'Yes, for Muriel.'

He shrugged, laughing uneasily. 'Oh I don't think we'll be making that much of a fuss over it,' he said. 'That would be a bit over the top, don't you think?'

Taken aback for a moment, she mumbled: 'Well, whatever you all think is . . . appropriate.'

'I mean, when this has happened before,' said Robert, 'we haven't bothered with a funeral or anything.'

'This has happened before?' she asked horrified.

CHRONOLOGY AND NARRATIVE

Another important aspect of how events are related is the sequence in which they are told: the **chronological narrative**. Crime fiction is one genre in particular where chronology is important. Does the story start with the body being discovered, the murder itself, the planning of the murder, the detective being called to the case and so on? And then what comes next? The way an author approaches chronology will have a profound effect on the sort of crime story that is written.

If we take as an example a typical plot line from a detective story, its chronological sequence might be something like:

1. A serial killer commits a number of murders.
2. A body is found which yields evidence.

3. The detective pursues a number of clues and identifies the killer.
4. A violent shoot-out leads to the death of the villain.

It is easy to conceive, however, other ways of presenting this sequence – for example, it could go 4, then 1, 2, 3 or 2, 1, 3, 4 and so on. In each case something different would be foregrounded by the chronology. Chronology, then, is one way in which the writer of a narrative can influence the way a reader responds to it. This can lead to a focus on suspense, where the action and its results are foregrounded, or on character, where feelings are foregrounded, or sometimes both.

Exercise 5

Go back to the rewritten story you used in exercise 3. Now try telling the story by changing its chronology. What aspects of the story become foregrounded by this change?

Exercise 6

The following telephone conversation, between Tod and Irene, is taken from Martin Amis's book *Time's Arrow*.

Bearing in mind the work done so far in this chapter, comment on the way Amis has constructed this conversation. Suggestions for answer on this exercise are at the back of the book.

> 'Goodbye, Tod.'
> 'Wait. Don't do anything.'
> 'Who cares? It's all shit anyway.'
> 'Irene,' he said.
> 'Yes I am Tod, I'm just this terrible old lady now. How'd it happen?'
> 'No you're not.'
> 'No I'm not. I'm going to kill myself.'
> 'No you're not.'
> 'I'm going to call the *New York Times*.'
> 'Irene, ' he said, with a new heat in his voice. And a new heat all over his body.
> 'I know you changed your name. How about that! I know you ran.'
> 'You know nothing.'
> 'I'm going to tell on you.'
> 'Oh yes?'
> 'You say it in the night. In your sleep.'
> 'Irene.'
> 'I know your secret.'
> 'What is it?'

> 'I want you to know something.'
> 'Irene, you're drunk.'
> 'Piece of shit.'
> 'Yes?' said Tod boredly – and hung up on her.

READER'S POINT OF VIEW

So far we have looked at some of the technical ways in which narrative works. Like many of the metaphorical terms used to describe aspects of narrative, such as 'focus' and 'perspective', the term 'point of view' comes from a way of seeing, and seeing is itself often used metaphorically to describe understanding. Recognising whose point of view is being placed in the foreground of a story gives the reader a greater sense of how the story can be understood and responded to.

The term 'point of view' has several uses, both in everyday speech and in the study of narrative. When we say something like 'it depends upon your point of view', we can mean (a) it depends upon where you are positioned in the argument (i.e. are you an employer or an employee?) and (b) it depends upon your personal beliefs and values. Both of these meanings of the term can be applied when looking at its role in narrative. It refers both to *where the narrative is focused at any given time*, and the *reader's responses to what is being presented*.

We have already seen in this chapter that there are various ways in which the narrative can be focused. This can lead to the following points of view being emphasised:

- The narrator's point of view
- A character's point of view

It must be remembered, though, that readers are involved in this process too, so we need to add to the list of points of view:

- The narratee's, or implied ideal reader's point of view

From this list it should be clear that we as readers can potentially have to sift through a range of points of view when reading a complex story. It is likely that we will come to see one or more of these as being preferred by the author over others. We may, though, choose to resist this preference because of our own attitudes and values. Borrowing terms often used in media studies, we can say that while the text may have a recognisable **dominant reading position**, we may wish to take an **oppositional reading position**.

Behind the points of view listed above, then, lie two more:

- The actual author's point of view
- The actual reader's point of view

It is not necessarily the case that these will coincide. One of the examples quoted earlier from *Bleak House* is a case in point.

> I have a great deal of difficulty in beginning to write my portion of these pages, for I know I am not clever. I always knew that. I used to say to my doll, when we were alone together, 'Now Dolly, I am not clever, you know very well, and you must be patient with me, like a dear!'

When we read the young woman's narrative, we soon work out that Dickens almost certainly means us to approve of what she says. In other words this is the dominant reading position. Modern readers, as we have already seen, are less likely to fall for her sentimentality. In the first instance we may look to see if Dickens is being ironic, if he is setting up a narrator who is meant to be questioned; when we fail to find such **irony**, some readers will begin to question their sympathy with her part of the story. This sense of opposition to a dominant reading position is one of the main ways in which multiple readings of texts are possible, often through exploring the context of a text's production and reception.

Exercise 7

The final exercise of this chapter will review a number of the issues that have been discussed in this chapter.

In the following two extracts from Alison Lurie's novel *The Last Resort*, the same episode is narrated twice. As readers, we have already been told that Professor Wilkie Walker, a famous naturalist, thinks he has a fatal illness, so has decided to commit suicide by drowning himself to save his wife Jenny from having to look after him. Jenny, though, knows none of this. Meanwhile a young woman called Barbie Mumpson, who is campaigning to save a rare creature called a manatee, is hugely impressed by Wilkie who she thinks can help with her campaign. As the twice-told event takes place, Wilkie has just had to abort his first attempt at suicide.

Referring to aspects of narrative highlighted in this chapter:

(a) Write a commentary on the narrative method used in each extract.
(b) Comment on the effect of the same episode being narrated twice.

In answering these questions consider in particular:

- Narrative focus
- Presentation of speech and thought
- What the reader knows compared to what the characters know
- Whether either character's point of view seems to be favoured

Suggestions for answer can be found at the back of the book.

Extract A

Dressed, she (Jenny) descended the stairs, glancing back out the window again. Wilkie was not on his way back from the beach now she saw. He was here already, standing by the gate in his swim trunks, talking to Barbie Mumpson, who stood close to him, looking up with the worshipful expression common to Wilkie's fans.

But as Jenny began to turn away from this familiar sight, something unfamiliar happened. Barbie stood on tiptoe, flung her arms around Wilkie, and kissed him full on the mouth. Occasionally in the past Jenny had seen overeager women try to do this, and her husband's reaction had always been a speedy though polite flinch of withdrawal. But now Wilkie did not withdraw; he might even have joined in, though it was hard to be sure. He just went on standing there.

And maybe nothing unfamiliar has happened, Jenny thought as Barbie finally let go of her husband: nothing that hasn't happened before. Maybe that's why Wilkie's been so strange lately, so distant. Maybe when he said last year that they were getting older, it was her age he was speaking of, not his own. He meant that Jenny no longer interested him romantically, that he wanted someone younger. Well, I'm not interested in you either, Jenny thought. I hate you.

Extract B

First he needed a hot shower and a shot of bourbon. The windows of their house were unlit: maybe nobody was home.

No such luck. There was a female figure by the gate, half illuminated by the outdoor lights that went on routinely at dusk. Not Jenny, but the friend of the manatee, Barbie Mumpson.

'Oh! Professor Walker!' she cried in a rush, grabbing his sore arm. 'I've been waiting for you, I've got so much to tell you! I met this really nice man on the beach this afternoon, and he says there's a lot of wonderful people in the Keys that are working to save the manatee. And I told him you might be interested, and they were absolutely thrilled. They're having a big meeting here next week, and I said I'd ask you to speak. So please, please say you will, because I promised I'd try as hard as I could –'

The girl stood close to Wilkie, clutching his injured arm, looking up at him with her round, stupid baby face, panting at him, blocking his way into the house. Get rid of her, he thought.

'Yes, all right,' he growled, because in two weeks he would no longer exist. Exhausted, he tried to put her aside, but Barbie wouldn't let go.

'Oh thank you, thank you!' she whined; and then suddenly she bounced up and planted a long wet, sloppy, warm kiss on his mouth.

SUMMARY

The following are the main points that have been established in this chapter:

- Many texts, and not just those defined as literary, have a narrative
- A narrative has a narrator and a narratee, but the real reader does not have to accept what the narratee is being encouraged to accept
- Narrative involves knowledge. The narrator knows and tells something that the narratee does not know
- A narrator at any one time is either first or third person
- All first person narratives must to an extent contain internal focus, because the narrator is bound to comment on their own thoughts and responses to situations and people
- Third person narratives can be more varied in their points of view across a story
- Narrators, especially first person narrators, are not always reliable in what they tell us
- Presenting speech and thought allows an author to develop character and move perspective
- The chronological sequence of a narrative means that certain aspects of the story can be highlighted
- Different points of view can be accepted or rejected by the reader

It must be stressed that not all of these are relevant all of the time, nor do they work in isolation.

REPRESENTING TALK

CHAPTER 5

This chapter will look at some aspects of the way talk is represented in literary texts. In conjunction with this chapter you should read Chapter 4 on narrative and point of view, which also looks at some of the implications behind the ways in which authors use talk.

In order to highlight some key issues about the way talk is represented in literature, it will be helpful first to compare an example of real-life talk and literary talk. In looking at an example of real-life talk, this should help to show the ways in which literary texts represent some of the ways in which people talk, rather than replicate them. It will also throw some light on the often used idea that certain kinds of talk in literature are somehow 'realistic'.

REAL-LIFE TALK AND LITERARY TALK

Exercise 1

Look closely at each of the two extracts which follow. Text A is a transcription of two young women talking. Text B is taken from the opening of the third act of Oscar Wilde's play *The Importance of Being Earnest*, where again two young women are talking.

Text A – Sue and Beth

B: Sue what are you doing Saturday (3) do you want to come to Shindig
S: oh I'm going clubbing on Thursday
B: just crush me why don't you (.) who with (.) WHO with
S: Ben
B: well can't he come to Shindig
S: think he's going away next week (3) I haven't got enough <u>money to</u>
B: <u>god he's never here</u>

(Source: Jessie Flynn: where text is underlined, both are speaking at the same time. Pauses are indicated in brackets)

Text B

(The scene is set in a manor house. Gwendolen and Cecily are being courted by Jack and Algernon, but have recently fallen out with them. At first hostile to each other, the two women are now temporarily friends.)

Gwendolen and Cecily are at the window, looking out into the garden.

GWENDOLEN: The fact that they did not follow us at once into the house, as any one else would have done, seems to me to show that they have some sense of shame left.

CECILY: They have been eating muffins. That looks like repentance.

GWENDOLEN (*after a pause*): They don't seem to notice us at all. Couldn't you cough.

CECILY: But I haven't got a cough.

GWENDOLEN: They're looking at us. What effrontery!

CECILY: They're approaching. That's very forward of them.

GWENDOLEN: Let us preserve a dignified silence.

CECILY: Certainly. It's the only thing to do now.

(a) With a partner, read each extract aloud as though performing for an audience.
(b) Then write notes on what seem to you to be the most distinctive features of each text as examples of talk.
(c) Based on these brief examples what can be established as broad distinctions between real-life talk, and the representation of such talk in stage drama?

Suggestions for Answer

The first point to note is that it probably proved impossible to 'perform' text A, certainly as it is shown here with its pauses and overlaps. You may have managed a version of this talk, but almost certainly you will have had to adapt the text to do so. This suggests that there is a fundamental difference between talk that happens in real life and talk that can be performed.

Text A, while an example of real-life talk, is nonetheless still a representation of such talk, because it is in the form of a transcript. Analysis of this transcript can be placed into two broad sections:

(a) Interactional features of the conversation.
(b) Contextual factors within the conversation.

In terms of interaction it is possible to look at issues such as who sets the agenda for the conversation and how that agenda is negotiated through aspects of talk such as methods of address, turn-taking, pauses and so on. Beth is establishing the agenda here in that she wants Sue to go out with her to a club on Saturday, but she does not ask this directly. She addresses her friend by name, which is strictly speaking unnecessary as they are the only two there, and she asks a preliminary question, followed by a pause, before she asks the real question directly. She is apparently allowing for and maybe even anticipating a negative answer.

And she does indeed get a negative answer, although again in an indirect way. When Sue says that she is 'going clubbing on Thursday', the pragmatic understanding here, which we as onlookers can probably work out, but which they as participants both clearly understand, is that Sue is not going out with Beth on Saturday. Instead she is going out on Thursday.

The first part of Beth's next utterance 'just crush me why don't you' is presumably voiced jokingly, although it may also show that Beth is indeed feeling some sort of rejection. Beth has one more go at asking Sue out, this time by suggesting Ben can come too. Again we can work out, at least partially, the pragmatics of Sue's answers here. Ben will be away by Saturday, or so she 'thinks', but this theoretically opens up the possibility she can go with Beth after all. Following a brief pause, therefore, Sue begins to use lack of money as a reason not to go out – she can't afford two nights out in the same week. Before she can finish, though, Beth introduces a topic change, and she does so by speaking at the same time as Sue. It would appear that Beth has conceded defeat, and is perhaps using the topic change to save embarrassment for both of them.

There are some contextual factors here which we can work out, and others which are more complex. We can work out that Shindig is the name of a club, and that Ben is Sue's boyfriend, for example. Much harder to work out from this extract is the exact nature of the relationship between the two women, although access to how they speak and look at each other would have added further valuable evidence. It would appear here that Beth seeks Sue's friendship, and that Sue is keeping Beth at some sort of distance, albeit in a considerate sort of way.

Text B is the text of a piece of stage drama, lines written to be delivered by actors who will, in each performance of the play, deliver them in different ways, however slight those differences may be. These differences will involve prosodic features such as intonation and emphasis. Unlike real-life talk, though, the lines will be delivered to an audience, a third party who must be able to understand what is going on. This means that some of the features noted in Text A above, such as overlaps, half-finished statements, pauses and so on cannot be reproduced in stage drama.

Drama scripts also involve aspects of **characterisation**. This means that the playwright is creating for the audience aspects of character through the spoken words. Although it can be said that we display aspects of our character through the way we talk in real life, such display of characteristics is not done with the speed and rapidity required of a two-hour play.

Whereas pragmatic understanding is often found in real-life talk, it is found less often in drama. Although it is possible, to an extent, to have pragmatic understanding at work in stage talk, it is only possible if the audience has been explicitly informed of issues earlier or if the characters are replicating understood social/cultural conventions.

Some playwrights and scriptwriters, especially more modern ones, try to represent qualities of real talk, but in the end that is what they are doing – *representing* real talk. Authors when writing talk can represent it in various ways, and with the collusion of the audience a version of reality is accepted. This means that the issues that we saw in Text A – broadly to do with interaction and context – can be found in stage drama, but they happen in very different ways.

Whereas the context of spontaneous talk is understood by the participants, but often needs to be guessed at by outsiders, context within drama is more clearly explained because of chronological narrative. In other words, things are made clear as we go along, especially at the start with the establishment of such things as time and place. By the time we reach Text B, which opens the final act of the play *The Importance of Being Earnest*, much of this context has been already established. We know the location, we know the two women and we know the 'they' whom they are talking about.

One job that this section of dialogue in Text B performs is to complement the action of the play. It is unlikely that two women talking would say in real talk 'they're approaching' – after all it would be obvious to both. The reason it is said here is for the sake of the audience, who need to know that the two men are about to appear on stage. Similarly, the reference to eating muffins is a reminder to the audience of how Act 2 closed, with Jack and Algernon indeed eating muffins. Although the line is meant to be comic, following up on other references to eating in the play, it also gives a sense of unity to the play, of action that is ongoing. Real talk rarely does things so neatly, partly because real talk does not usually have an audience outside those taking part, and so only needs to work for those who are taking part.

A similar sort of neatness can be seen in the women's interaction too. Relationships are more clearly defined, even in this brief extract. It is Gwendolen who sets the agenda here, talking of what the 'fact' shows, and telling Cecily to cough. Cecily is not to be ordered around, though, and her 'But I haven't got a cough' is not so much her being literal, as refusing to be bossed about.

What we have found, then, from these two starting points are the following:

- Real-life talk is in many ways different from talk in drama
- Real-life talk is less neatly shaped than its dramatic representation but makes sense to the participants

- Both types of talk rely on contextual factors, but they work differently in each
- The needs of an audience affect the way talk is represented in drama
- The requirements of story-telling also affect the way talk is represented in drama

DIALOGUES

Fictional Dialogues: Prose

Dialogue forms an important part of many texts which create an illusion of the real world by representing it fictionally. Most stage drama is heavily or totally dependent upon dialogue for its effect, as is radio drama and, to a lesser extent, film and television. Most prose fiction contains at least some dialogue.

As its most basic point this chapter is aiming to show you that real-life talk is not the same as its representation in literature. This means that when critics say such things as 'Writer X has a wonderful ear for dialogue' or 'Novel X captures perfectly the way people speak', these comments cannot be taken literally. A writer may be very good at giving the *illusion* of real speech, but this is as far as it goes. This is not to say that writers set out to achieve a goal which they fail to meet, that literary dialogue is inferior to the real thing. It is just different.

Exercise 2

The first piece of prose-fiction dialogue to be examined will look at the way dialogue contributes to characterisation, in this example to the establishment of a character very early in a novel. In the first two chapters of *Hard Times* Charles Dickens introduces Mr Thomas Gradgrind, a man who is in no doubt that he is right in everything that he does. Here Mr Gradgrind inspects a class at the local school. Read the extract carefully and then make notes on the following:

1. What is the nature of the interaction presented here by Dickens?
2. In what ways is Mr Gradgrind's character presented by Dickens?
3. How are the two pupils, Sissy Jupe and Bitzer, characterised through the way they speak?

Text: *Hard Times*

'Girl number twenty,' said Mr. Gradgrind, squarely pointing with his square forefinger, 'I don't know that girl. Who is that girl?'

'Sissy Jupe, Sir,' explained number twenty, blushing, standing up, and curtseying.

'Sissy is not a name,' said Mr. Gradgrind. 'Don't call yourself Sissy. Call yourself Cecilia.'

'It's father as calls me Sissy, Sir,' returned the young girl in a trembling voice, and with another curtsey.

'Then he had no business to do it,' said Mr. Gradgrind. 'Tell him he mustn't. Cecilia Jupe. Let me see. What is your father?'

'He belongs to the horse-riding, if you please, Sir.'

Mr. Gradgrind frowned and waved off the objectionable calling with his hand.

'We don't want to know anything about that here. You mustn't tell us about that, here. Your father breaks horses, don't he?'

'If you please, Sir, when they can get any to break, they do break horses in the ring, Sir.'

'You mustn't tell us about the ring, here. Very well, then. Describe your father as a horsebreaker. He doctors sick horses, I dare say?'

'Oh yes, Sir.'

'Very well then. He is a veterinary surgeon, a farrier, and a horsebreaker. Give me your definition of a horse.'

(Sissy Jupe thrown into the greatest alarm by this demand.)

'Girl number twenty unable to define a horse!' said Mr. Gradgrind, for the general behoof of all the little pitchers. 'Girl number twenty possessed of no facts, in reference to one of the commonest of animals! Some boy's definition of a horse. Bitzer, yours.' . . .

'Bitzer,' said Thomas Gradgrind. 'Your definition of a horse.'

'Quadruped. Graminivorous. Forty teeth, namely twenty-four grinders, four eye-teeth, and twelve incisive. Sheds coat in the spring; in marshy countries, sheds hoofs, too. Hoofs hard, but requiring to be shod with iron. Age known by marks in mouth.' Thus (and much more) Bitzer.

Suggestions for Answer

The interaction here is between a teacher, or strictly speaking an inspector, and pupils. It has a number of ingredients, all of them initiated by Gradgrind. He asks questions, he makes pronouncements and he issues commands. Note how many verb forms give negative orders: 'don't', 'mustn't' in particular. Whereas he addresses the pupils variously by number, full name and surname only, Sissy Jupe repeatedly calls him 'Sir'. His power is absolute.

This absolute power, though, is used by Gradgrind to bully Sissy. He points with his square forefinger, he demands the girl change her name, he objects to her father's occupation. Anything that smacks of imagination, such as a cute name or the father working in the circus, is to be denied. He demands facts and definitions that suit his pre-arranged ideas, nothing else will do. He is utterly in command of his world and although there is a certain grim humour in the way it is done, it is a frighteningly rigid world he represents.

Sissy is presented as a timid and rather bemused girl. She does not rebel: she just cannot see what Gradgrind requires. Bitzer – another name which suggests personal qualities, in this case hardness – can define a horse, though, by speaking like a reference book.

This piece of dialogue establishes different sets of values. On the one hand we have Gradgrind and his square functional world of facts and definitions, supported by the brainwashed Bitzer who has learnt the rules; on the other hand we have Sissy Jupe with her pretty name, her innocence, her inability even to understand the question she is being asked.

Exercise 3

The second example of prose-fiction dialogue comes from James Lee Burke's novel *Purple Cane Road* (2000). Detective Dave Robicheaux is hunting a hitman, and suspects that the hitman, operating under an assumed name, has befriended his daughter, Alafair. Alafair is at a creative writing class, and Robicheaux, sensing that she is in danger, goes to collect her. This is a first person narrative, narrated by Dave Robicheaux, and the extract starts as Alafair sees her father at the door.

Read the extract at least twice and then make notes on the following question:

How does Burke present the dialogue in terms of who is speaking and how, and any accompanying physical actions?

> '*Dave . . .,*' she said, the word almost twisting as it came out of her mouth.
> 'The kid who paints ceramics? Is he here tonight?' I said.
> She squeezed here eyes shut, as though in pain, and opened them again. 'I knew that was it.'
> 'Alf, this guy isn't what you think he is. He's a killer for hire. He's the guy who escaped custody in the shoot-out on the Atchafalaya.'
> 'No, you're wrong. His name is Jack O'Roarke. He's not a criminal. He paints beautiful things. He showed me photographs of the things he's done.'
> 'That's the guy. O'Roarke was his father's name. Where is he?'
> A fan oscillated behind her head; her eyes were moist and dark inside the skein of hair that blew around her face.
> 'It's a mistake of some kind. He's an artist. He's a gentle person. Jack wouldn't hurt anybody,' she said.
> 'Alf, come with me,' I said and put my hand on her forearm, my fingers closing around the skin, harder than I meant to.
> 'No, I'm not going anywhere with you. You're humiliating me.'

> I could see the veins in her forearm bunched like blue string under the skin, and I released her and realized my hand was shaking now.
>
> 'I'm sorry,' I said.
>
> 'Everybody's looking at us. Just go,' she said, her voice lowered, as though she could trap her words in the space between the two of us.
>
> 'He's here isn't he?'
>
> 'I'll never forgive you for this.'

Suggestions for Answer

Because Robicheaux is narrating this exchange, we are told far more about his daughter's appearance and actions than about his. It is as though we are seeing what he is seeing, and because we as readers know the danger Alafair is in, we share his concern for her. We are also told twice about her voice, about how she speaks, but are not told about how Robicheaux speaks his words. This is because we do not need to be told – we can anticipate the anxiety which in a sense we share.

Most students are told at some time in their education that constantly repeating the word 'said' leads to monotonous writing; it is much better to add an adverb as 'he said quietly' or to use one of the many variants of 'said' such as 'he whispered'. This is not the case here, though, where 'she said' and 'I said' are the only words used to identify who is speaking. There is a reason for this. The plain word 'said' communicates the urgency and seriousness of the conversation which would be lost if Burke had used a more varied method.

In addition to his use of 'said' Burke at times lets the conversation move forward without saying who is speaking – in other words he uses free speech. (See Chapter 4.) With two people speaking in turns, the reader is able to keep track of who is speaking without always being told.

Here, then, Burke creates a sense of urgency not just through what is said, but by careful control of the narrative point of view and by careful management of the descriptive language which accompanies prose dialogue.

Fictional Dialogues: Stage Drama

It has already been stressed that real-life talk is not the same as its representation in literature. With drama in particular, though, it is often suggested that the representation of talk gets very close to the real thing. There is an obvious reason for this, in that the dialogue that is presented on stage, and even to an extent on the scripted page, is not mediated by narrative description, unless perhaps stage directions are included – these stage directions exist only in the text version, though, not in the version that is performed. Despite the claims that are sometimes made for the 'reality' of stage talk, the fact remains that as soon as a writer puts pen to paper and creates fictional dialogue, that is what it is – fictional.

One playwright who is often said to write 'realistic' dialogue is Harold Pinter. Writing in 1968 the critic Ronald Hayman said:

> Pinter has capitalised . . . on the fact that real-life conversations don't proceed smoothly and logically from point to point. Conventional characters in conventional plays listen to each other intently and answer each other intelligently, but it is only a tiny minority of people who do this in reality. The average everyday conversation is repetitious or inconsequential or both; Pinter has an accurate and affectionate ear for the irrationality of dialogue . . .
>
> (*Harold Pinter*, Ronald Hayman, Heinemann)

Before looking at the extract from Pinter that Hayman goes on to quote, some issues he raises need to be questioned. The linguist H. P. Grice set out, in what are sometimes known as Grice's Maxims, some so-called rules of conversation. Although these often oversimplify matters, they are broadly speaking helpful in looking at real-life talk. He said that when we are in a conversation which is co-operative, as most are, we try to (a) be as specific as possible when we speak, and only give as much information as we need to; (b) tell the truth; (c) be relevant; and (d) make our meaning clear. Grice's maxims of real-life talk clearly differ from what Hayman says about it.

Exercise 4

Read carefully the following extract from Pinter's review sketch entitled *Last to Go*, first performed in 1959. The character labelled MAN is a newspaper seller, talking at a coffee bar to BARMAN after he has sold all of his papers.

Make notes on the following task:

Referring back to the work done on real-life talk at the beginning of this chapter (see exercise 1) is it possible to agree with Hayman that Pinter's dialogue is like 'everyday average conversation'?

Suggestions for answer can be found at the back of the book.

MAN:	I went to see if I could get hold of George.
BARMAN:	Who?
MAN:	George.
(Pause)	
BARMAN:	George who?
MAN:	George . . . whatsisname.

BARMAN:	Oh.
(Pause)	
	Did you get hold of him?
MAN:	No. No, I couldn't get hold of him. I couldn't locate him.
BARMAN:	He's not about much now, is he?
(Pause)	
MAN:	When did you last see him then?
BARMAN:	Oh, I haven't seen him for years.
MAN:	No, nor me.
(Pause)	
BARMAN:	Used to suffer very bad from arthritis.
MAN:	Arthritis?
BARMAN:	Yes.
MAN:	He never suffered from arthritis.
BARMAN:	Suffered very bad.
(Pause)	
MAN:	Not when I knew him.
(Pause)	
BARMAN:	I think he must have left the area.
(Pause)	
MAN:	Yes, it was the *Evening News* was the last to go tonight.
BARMAN:	Not always the last though, is it, though?
MAN:	No. Oh no. I mean sometimes it's the *News*. Other times it's one of the others. No way of telling beforehand. Until you've got your last one left, of course. Then you can tell which one it's going to be.
BARMAN:	Yes.
(Pause)	
MAN:	Oh yes.
(Pause)	
	I think he must have left the area.

MONOLOGUES

There are many types of spoken monologue which occur in real life, all of which have distinctive features. These distinctive features are in part a result of conventions and in part due to the nature of the audience, even if technically the audience is either not there at all or not 'allowed' to speak. Some examples of such monologues include speaking to an answerphone message, talking to your pet, saying 'Whoops!' when tripping over a paving stone. More public monologues include addressing a school assembly, reading the news, making a political speech. In each case the monologue is conditioned by various contexts, such as the technology being used, the potential audience for the monolgue, whether it is scripted and so on.

While all of the monologues mentioned above involve only one speaker, with no spoken interaction with anyone else, it should nonetheless be clear that the audience for these monologues – either physically present at the speech event or 'present' in a more remote sense – have a considerable influence on what is being said. This audience can range from a very particular one in the case of the answerphone, to a much more general one in the case of the newsreader, but in all cases the nature of the likely audience affects what is said.

The word 'audience' is used here to refer to those who are the intended receivers of a speech act. If we turn now to literary monologues, literary in the sense that they are pre-written and then performed in front of people, the word 'audience' takes on a different dimension. The audience for a play, especially a stage play for which they have bought a ticket, are committed in most cases to being an homogenous group of people who sit quietly until given their cues to respond. They know that what they are watching is a performance.

It has already been stressed that literary texts are a representation of reality, and in one sense, therefore, any of the sorts of real-life monologue shown above can appear represented in a novel or play. A character in a novel or play can speak to her dog, or give a speech and, if she happens to be a weather forecaster by trade, do a weather forecast. In each case, though, the literary effect of representation will produce something different from real-life talk.

Monologues in Novels

One of the first things we notice when reading a novel is its **narrative voice**. A simple distinction of **narrative voice** is between third person and first person, although within these broad categories there are many subtle distinctions. In most first person narratives, the narrator is a character who tells the story without showing any sense of who the story is being told to, or indeed why it is being told. In one sense, then, such novels have similarities with dramatic monologues, but they rarely have the sense of being written to be spoken, in the way drama is.

There are, though, some exceptions, where authors do try to create a sense of a narrative that is being spoken. If they are to create this illusion of a spoken narrative, then they need to create an audience the narrator is speaking to.

Exercise 5

A modern example of this effect can be seen in Julian Barnes's novel *Love, etc.* (2000). This novel is in the form of various characters speaking aloud, the same characters who were first seen in Barnes's novel *Talking it Over* (1991). Here Barnes confronts head-on the problem of who the audience for a monologue is by addressing a narratee directly. This technique of having characters 'talk' directly to a reader or narratee is still, though, a fictional representation of talk – and we of course cannot reply, even if the characters suggest that we have in some way responded. The following is the first 'speech' in the novel.

In what ways does this extract suggest that Stuart is having a conversation with someone?

> **Stuart**
>
> Hello!
>   We've met before. Stuart. Stuart Hughes.
>   Yes, I am sure. Positive. About ten years ago.
>   It's all right – it happens. You don't have to pretend. But the point is, I remember *you*. I'd hardly forget, would I? A bit over ten years, now I come to think of it.
>   Well, I've changed. Sure. This is all grey for a start. Can't even call it pepper-and-salt any more, can I?
>   Oh, and by the way, *you've* changed too. You probably think you're pretty much the same as you were back then. Believe me, you aren't.
>
> (*Love, etc.*, Julian Barnes: Jonathan Cape, 2000)

Suggestions for Answer

One method used is the idea that the supposed reader has interrupted the monologue: when Stuart says, 'Yes, I am sure,' there is a sense that the reader has said that they do not know who Stuart is. Another is the direct address to the reader by using the pronoun 'you'. This is further enhanced by the suggestion that the reader is actually there, that '*you*'ve changed too'. The same effect that someone is being spoken to is created by using an **unreferenced pronoun** in 'This is all grey for a start.' The 'this' could be anything, but the contextual clues of age and colour make it clear enough that Stuart is indicating his hair.

This, then, is a monologue in that we can only read/hear the words of one character. If we insert the words that we as readers are implied to have said, however, the extract is much more like a dialogue.

Monologues in Shakespeare

Anyone with even a small amount of familiarity with Shakespeare's work will know that in many of his plays he uses what are known as soliloquies. Although the Latin derivation of the word soliloquy suggests 'solo speaker', what is usually being represented is the thoughts of a character being spoken aloud. This is, of course, like no 'speech' that we actually encounter in our everyday lives. We might occasionally, and to huge embarrassment on all sides, catch someone talking to themselves, but this is very different from thought, which is by definition unspoken.

Indeed, in Shakespeare's plays some of the best-known speeches are soliloquies. Although we have never seen our thoughts written down, we probably have an idea that thought is pretty random and unshaped. Yet just about the most famous line in all literature is, within the world of the play *Hamlet*, actually a thought:

'To be, or not to be, that is the question.'

If nothing else, the formal organisation of this line shows the extent to which literature represents the language we use rather than replicates it.

Another aspect of the soliloquy concerns its 'truth', truth that is within the context of the play. Whereas it is perfectly possible to lie in speech, surely your thoughts have to be 'true', what you honestly think, however confused you may be. Although this is usually the accepted convention when dealing with soliloquies, occasionally problems do arise. What if, for instance, over a number of soliloquies the speaker appears to contradict himself, as happens with Iago in *Othello*? Are we to assume that this congenital liar is lying to himself, to us the audience, or that somehow he's schizophrenic?

Exercise 6

The following two examples of a soliloquy are taken from Shakespeare's *Much Ado About Nothing*. Benedick and Beatrice, who appear to loathe each other, have sworn never to marry. Each is tricked by their friends into believing that the other is madly in love with them. And on believing this, they each then realise that they are actually in love with each other. There are two scenes in the play when the tricks are played, and each scene ends with a soliloquy from the character who has previously been hiding from friends, but is seen by the audience.

When you have read both texts, answer the following questions:

(a) How do these speeches suggest that the characters are working out their thoughts, rather than merely recording them?
(b) In what sense is it possible to say who these characters are actually speaking to?

Some suggestions for answers are at the back of the book.

Benedick

This can be no trick, the conference was sadly borne, they have the truth of this from Hero, they seem to pity the lady: it seems her affections have their full bent: love me? Why it must be requited: I hear how I am censured, they say I will bear myself proudly, if I perceive the love come from her: they say too, that she will rather die than give any sign of affection: I did never think to marry, I must not seem proud, happy are they that hear their detractions, and can put them to mending . . .

> **Beatrice**
>
> What fire is in mine ears? Can this be true?
> Stand I condemned for pride and scorn so much?
> Contempt, farewell, and maiden pride, adieu,
> No glory lives behind the back of such.
> And Benedick, love on, I will requite thee,
> Taming my wild heart to thy loving hand:
> If thou dost love, my kindness shall incite thee
> To bind our loves up in a holy band,
> For others say thou dost deserve, and I
> Believe it better than reportingly.

DEMOTIC SPEECH

One feature of real-life talk that authors sometimes try to simulate is regional and/or social variation from standard English. This representation of what is sometimes called **demotic** speech can be examined in a number of ways:

- It can be looked at technically – the ways in which the author when writing has tried to represent a particular accent and dialect can be analysed
- It can be looked at in terms of characterisation, placing characters as belonging to certain social groups and/or types
- It can be looked at in terms of representing certain attitudes and values which readers may be encouraged to approve or not

It should also be remembered that such speech in drama has the added impact of being heard by an audience when the play is performed. Indeed, it is perfectly possible for a director/actor to add a regional accent to a role which is not explicitly stated in the printed text version.

Exercise 7

Shaw's play *Pygmalion* is a play about speech and social class, so it is to be expected that he will attempt to represent regional speech in some of the characters; one such character is Alfred Doolittle who is described by Shaw as 'an elderly but vigorous dustman'. At the point in the play where the following extract is taken, Doolittle has had a makeover and is dressed 'resplendently as for a fashionable wedding'. He is, though, unhappy at the changes that have been made to his lifestyle by Henry Higgins and his friends. (NB Shaw does not use apostrophes for some shortened forms in this play.)

Read the following speech carefully and answer the following questions:

(a) In what ways does Shaw represent cockney dialect in the way Doolittle speaks?
(b) To what extent can Shaw be said to be representing social attitudes and values here?

Some suggestions for answer are at the back of the book.

> DOOLITTLE: Who asked him to make a gentleman of me? I was happy. I was free. I touched pretty nigh everybody for money when I wanted it, same as I touched you, Enry Iggins. Now I am worrited; tied neck and heels; and everybody touches me for money. It's a fine thing for you, says my solicitor. Is it? says I. You mean it's a good thing for you, I says . . . A year ago I hadnt a relative in the world except for two or three who wouldnt speak to me. Now Ive fifty, and not a decent week's wages among the lot of them. I have to live for others and not for myself: thats middle class morality.

SUMMARY

This chapter has done the following:

- Explored differences between 'real' talk and represented talk
- Analysed fictional dialogue in novels, drama and Shakespearean drama
- Analysed monologues in drama and novels
- Explored issues around the representation of demotic talk

CREATIVITY

This chapter will explore some aspects of creativity in literature, in particular metaphor and intertextuality.

The term 'creative writing', which is used in English courses ranging from school to university, usually refers to writing which takes the form of stories, poems and plays. The word 'creative' is attached to such writing because it is seen as doing something new, either new in its ideas and what it is saying, or new in its techniques of writing, or both. There are, of course, degrees to this. Some writers blaze across the sky, dazzling with their novelty; others are less obviously 'different' from what has gone before. But, whether it be through the invention of a completely new form of story-telling, or the subtle use of metaphors, it is expected that good writers will surprise their readers by doing things with language that have not been encountered before.

This sometimes means that creativity is often seen as a feature of literature only. Before looking at the way language is used creatively in literary texts, though, it needs to be stressed that creativity can be seen in many other uses of language too. In the companion volume to this book, *How Texts Work*, the chapter on literary/non-literary texts makes it clear that the distinction often made between these two types of text is not in fact as clear-cut as is often thought. If we understand that creativity with language surrounds us in an everyday sense, it should make it easier to analyse creativity in literature.

Exercise 1

The following are newspaper headlines:

- When a former prison officer was sent to prison, one newspaper used the headline *The Shaming of the Screw*
- A report on poor wages for hospital workers was headlined *All work and low pay*
- When an eye hospital was moved to a new building, a newspaper headline read *Site for sore eyes*

Write a short analysis of each of these headlines, describing how they play with language. There is no commentary with this exercise.

Linguists like to categorise, and one of the main things about creativity is that it deliberately breaks outside categories. So, with a warning that this is not an inclusive list, the following are some of the broad areas within which writers can do something new with language.

Lexical creativity: This operates at the level of single words and phrases. Examples would be invented new words, or old words used in new contexts.

Phonological creativity: This operates on the level of sound, and can involve repetition of sounds, playing with similar sounds but different meanings and so on.

Graphological creativity: This depends upon the design of a text creating an impact on the reader. The expected and conventional layout of a text can be altered in various ways.

Semantic creativity: Semantics is concerned with meaning, and one of the most obvious ways in which writers and speakers play with meaning is by using puns. At a deeper level, some twentieth-century writers have challenged the possibility of finding any meaning at all.

Grammatical creativity: Grammar involves the system and structure of a language, and so is less likely to be played with than some of the other levels of language use – deviating from the rules of **grammar** can make texts impossible to understand. Nonetheless writers will sometimes briefly suspend the rules of **grammar** to make a particular impact.

Metaphor: Metaphor and other terms for comparison are sometimes called figures of speech, because this categorisation is based upon classical rhetoric. A detailed look at metaphor will follow in this chapter.

Intertextual reference to other texts: It has already been noted that creativity with language often depends upon readers having prior knowledge of something. This prior knowledge allows writers to use a range of techniques, confident that at least some of their readers will understand what is going on. This intertextual reference can range from **allusion** – a passing reference to another text – to a much more significant use of imitation, such as **parody** and **satire**. A further look at intertextual reference will follow in this chapter.

METAPHOR

The word 'metaphor' comes from the Greek word *metaphora*, which means 'a transfer'. This idea of transferring can be explained by saying that if two things have certain characteristics in common, one can be described in terms of the other. When we most want to stress an idea, when we want to make a point forcefully, we tend to use metaphorical rather than literal language. In other words, when we want to say how something is, we say how it isn't! The act of comparison draws attention to the point being made.

Metaphors we Live by

The linguists G. Lakoff and M. Johnson, in their book *Metaphors We Live By* (1980) have indicated just how much of our language is metaphorical and that sometimes these metaphors become extended to show a whole way of thinking about something. Take, for example, the way your learning in a class or lecture is described in terms of a journey:

> The lesson begins
> You make a start
> You either make progress, even racing ahead . . .
> Or you lag behind the rest and get stuck . . .
> Or you could be getting nowhere . . .
> Or even going round in circles . . .
> But then you move on to the next topic
> And it is all very straightforward
> So you get through the exam
> And then you finish

Only when you really think about it do these terms become obvious as metaphors. Andrew Goatly in his book *The Language of Metaphors* (1997) describes these metaphors as 'inactive', suggesting that one way in which they have lost their original force is through being 'lexicalised'; in other words they have been defined in dictionaries with their new meanings.

Exercise 2

One of the most commonly used metaphors in everyday language is to describe understanding in terms of seeing. Make a list of words and phrases which use this comparison. There is no definitive list, but here are a few suggestions to get you started:

> You get the picture
> You see their point
> You search for an answer

The work so far on metaphors in everyday life should have helped you to think about the way in which metaphors appear in language. Much of our language is metaphorical, but with many forms of literature there is the expectation that the metaphors will be original, that the authors will show us a new way of seeing things.

Metaphors in Poetry

This chapter will now move on to work with some examples of metaphors in poetry.

Exercise 3

The following is the first verse of an untitled poem by AE Housman, first published in 1896. What metaphorical comparison is made here?

> Loveliest of trees, the cherry now
> Is hung with bloom along the bough
> And stands about the woodland ride
> Wearing white for Eastertide.

Suggestions for Answer

It should be relatively straightforward to see that the idea of a tree 'wearing white' is metaphorical: the tree is compared to a human dressing up. It could be argued that the idea that the tree 'stands' has already introduced this idea, and even the idea of the tree being 'hung with bloom' could be seen as part of the same process.

Exercise 4

The poem 'Dover Beach' by Matthew Arnold was published in 1867. One contextual reading of this poem is that it reflects on the loss of faith which many intellectuals experienced after the publication of Darwin's *On the Origin of Species* in 1859. In the poem Arnold uses each of the stanzas to advance his ideas, using as part of this process metaphorical language in a number of ways.

Read the poem carefully and make notes on the following questions, which take each stanza in turn, and then asks for a summary. Suggestions for answer can be found at the back of the book.

1. This stanza sets the physical scene by what can be seen. What use does Arnold make of metaphor here?
2. This stanza describes what can be heard. What use does Arnold make of metaphor here?
3. This stanza refers to the Greek philosopher Sophocles and his reflections on the sound of the Aegean Sea, before linking his ideas with his/our own. In what way does Arnold use a very explicit comparison here?
4. This stanza develops the idea from stanza 3 by using a complex network of images. Identify these images and try to work out what meanings can be found in them.
5. This stanza completes the poem by offering love as the only alternative to a world without faith. Identify the metaphorical language used here and say what interpretations are possible of the final three lines.
6. Looking at your answers so far, how has Arnold used metaphor as part of his overall process here?

Dover Beach

The sea is calm tonight,
The tide is full, the moon lies fair
Upon the straits; – on the French coast the light
Gleams and is gone; the cliffs of England stand,
Glimmering and vast, out in the tranquil bay.
Come to the window, sweet is the night-air!

Only, from the long line of spray
Where the sea meets the moon-blanch'd land,
Listen! you hear the grating roar
Of pebbles which the waves draw back, and fling
At their return, up the high strand,
Begin, and cease, and then begin again,
With tremulous cadence slow, and bring
The eternal note of sadness in.

Sophocles long ago
Heard it on the Aegean, and it brought
Into his mind the turbid ebb and flow
Of human misery; we
Find also in the sound a thought,
Hearing it by this distant northern sea.

The Sea of Faith
Was once, too, at the full, and round earth's shore
Lay like the folds of a bright girdle furl'd.
But now I only hear
Its melancholy, long, withdrawing roar,
Retreating, to the breath
Of the night-wind, down to the vast edges drear
And naked shingles of the world.

Ah, love, let us be true
To one another! for the world, which seems
To lie before us like a land of dreams,
So various, so beautiful, so new,
Hath really neither joy, nor love, nor light,
Nor certitude, nor peace, nor help for pain;
And we are here as on a darkling plain
Swept with confused alarms of struggle and flight,
Where ignorant armies clash by night.

ALLEGORY

Allegory is when a whole text can be seen to have a different possible meaning, and allegory is especially associated with religious and moral texts such as fables. The problem with allegory, though, is that because the whole text is potentially a comparison, at no point in the text itself is the point of comparison made clear. In many of Aesop's fables this problem is got over by an explicit addition to the text. At the end of the fable called *Look before you Leap* is the statement 'A sensible person never embarks upon an enterprise until they can see their way clear to the end of it.' This overt explanation, though, does tend to take away from the texts the ambiguity which can make allegory so interesting.

Exercise 5

The poem below by William Blake is allegorical. Read it through and answer the questions which follow. Suggestions for answer are at the back of the book.

The Garden of Love

I went to the Garden of Love
And saw what I never had seen:
A chapel was built in the midst,
Where I used to play on the green.

And the gates of this chapel were shut,
And 'Thou shalt not' writ over the door;
So I turn'd to the Garden of Love
That so many sweet flowers bore;

And I saw it was filled with graves,
And tomb-stones where flowers should be;
And priests in black gowns were walking their rounds,
And binding with briars my joys and desires.

1. Allegory often involves the creation of a fictional place. What is the fictional place here, and how is its importance signalled to the reader?
2. The speaker of the poem says that there have been changes to the Garden since he was last there. What are these changes?
3. In what way does the last line of the poem add a new dimension to what has been said before?
4. Putting all the evidence together, what interpretation of the allegory can you come up with?

INTERTEXTUALITY

Broadly speaking, intertextuality is the process by which texts make reference to other texts. In a chapter on creativity it may seem surprising to find a section based upon the use of texts already in existence, but there are ways in which this intertextual process can be seen as creatively interesting, not least because they involve using the reader's knowledge for the effects to work. Intertextual references abound in all sorts of texts, including films, cartoons, adverts, as well as literary texts.

However 'realistic' a text may seem as we read it, what we are reading is a representation of reality, rather than reality itself. (For a more detailed exploration of this idea see Chapter 1 of the companion volume to this called *How Texts Work*.) This representation is based upon various agreed systems, and the more experienced we become as readers, the more experience we have of how texts work in our culture. In this sense, then, all texts are intertextual for us as readers, because we draw on our experience of other texts every time we read.

Texts can be linked by genre, including the transformation from one genre to another, through parody or by specific allusion. A source text can be transformed by a new writer, adding new characters and themes, or even rewritten from a new perspective.

Intertextuality can also be used as a concept to explore the ways in which some writers are different from the mainstream, this difference being a reaction against convention, but nonetheless dependent on convention for the shock effect. The dialect poetry of Burns and others is a rejection of conventional standard English as the medium of poetry, for example.

Look again at Chapter 3, Exercise 3, to see how intertextual references are used in the advertisement for the Terry Pratchett Discworld novel.

Exercise 6

The exercise which follows completes this chapter on creativity by illustrating an 'unusual' piece of writing. The extract is taken from the opening of the novel *Motherless Brooklyn* by Jonathan Lethem. The story is narrated by a character named Lionel who suffers from the brain disorder known as Tourette's syndrome. People who have this disorder suffer from involuntary tics, and especially uncontrollable speech, in which they blurt things out without being able to stop.

Look at the extract overleaf and comment on the ways in which the author represents this condition in Lionel's narrative. Suggestions for answer can be found at the back of the book.

Context is everything. Dress me up and see. I'm a carnival barker, an auctioneer, a downtown performance artist, a speaker in tongues, a senator drunk on filibuster. *I've got Tourette's.* My mouth won't quit, though mostly I whisper or subvocalise like I'm reading aloud, my Adam's apple bobbing, jaw muscle beating like a miniature heart under my cheek, the noise suppressed, the words escaping silently, mere ghosts of themselves, husks empty of breath and tone. (If I were a Dick Tracy villain, I'd have had to be Mumbles.) In this diminished form the words rush out of the cornucopia of my brain to course over the surface of the world, tickling reality like fingers on piano keys. Caressing, nudging. They're an invisible army on a peace-keeping mission, a peaceable horde. They mean no harm. They placate, interpret, massage. Everywhere they're smoothing down imperfections, putting hairs in place, putting ducks in a row, replacing divots. Counting and polishing the silver. Patting old ladies gently on the behind, eliciting a giggle. Only – here's the rub – when they find too much perfection, when the surface is already buffed smooth, the ducks already orderly, the old ladies complacent, then my little army rebels, breaks into stores. Reality needs a prick here and there, the carpet needs a flaw. My words begin plucking at threads nervously, seeking purchase, a weak point, a vulnerable ear. That's when it comes, the urge to shout in the church, the nursery, the crowded movie house. It's an itch at first. Inconsequential. But that itch is soon a torrent behind a straining dam. Noah's flood. That itch is my whole life. Here it comes now. Cover your ears. Build an ark.

'Eat me!' I scream.

SUMMARY

This chapter has done the following:

- Explored notions of creativity in literary and non-literary texts
- Described different types of creativity
- Explored issues around metaphor and allegory
- Described some aspects of intertextuality

THE FRAMEWORK REVISITED

Chapters 2–6 have explored each category of the framework first seen in Chapter 1. As was pointed out there, these are fairly crude divisions, which often overlap and appear simultaneously in literary texts. The framework is useful, though, in identifying possible areas to look at when answering the question 'How does a text work?'

When working under the pressure of timed examinations it is always helpful to have a structure to fall back on. Learning the following categories, and applying them sensibly to individual texts and extracts will allow you to analyse the language of literature, whether the text has already been studied in class, or whether it is being seen for the first time in an exam.

Shapes and patterns (see Chapter 2): Look for titles, openings and closings, the connections between parts of the text. Look also at patterns of repeated words, repeated sounds (alliteration, assonance, rhyme etc.), repeated grammar structures, semantic fields (i.e. words which cluster around the same area of meaning).

Genre (see Chapter 3): Look for how whole texts fit into genres, how texts relate to other texts. Consider genre in terms of its shape/form, and in terms of its content. Consider the ways in which genre can be subverted, by mixing, for example inappropriate content and form.

Narrative (see Chapter 4): Look for the voices which 'speak' the texts, how much they know, their reliability, shifting narrators, the role of the reader in identifying narrative point of view, irony.

Voices in texts (see Chapter 5): Look for the voices which speak in texts, such as characters in drama, dialogue in novels. Consider the use of different levels of formality, regional speech and so on.

Creativity and play (see Chapter 6): Look for metaphors and comparisons and work out what they contribute to meanings. Look for multiple meanings and how they are created. Look for ways in which authors use language in a consciously creative way, such as by using archaic words, inventing 'new' words, breaking grammatical rules, using unusual graphology, playing with words and meanings, creating ambiguity, suggesting absence – what is not in the text but might be expected to be, making intertextual references.

SUGGESTIONS FOR ANSWER

CHAPTER 1, EXERCISE 3

When you are asked to compare texts, you are essentially looking at *similarity* and *difference*. In terms of similarity, we can begin by noting that both poems have the same title, a fact which means that they are meant to be seen as two poems to be taken together. This poem has many of the same sound qualities seen in the first poem, such as rhyme, repetition, and it actually reuses parts of the first two stanzas of the original poem. The opening two lines of each second stanza are identical.

The more significant aspects of comparison, though, are usually found in difference. This poem is only two stanzas long and this time appears to contain only one voice. There is no debate about the children coming home. There are fewer words suggesting sound, and instead of 'laughing' being heard on the hill, it is now 'whisp'rings' being heard in the dale. Whispering is a controlled form of talk, and is also the talk of rumour and malice.

The single voice of the poem, the nurse presumably, draws on her own experience of life to give the children a grim view of the future. In the first stanza she says that

> The days of my youth rise fresh in my mind:
> My face turns green and pale.

Literally for a face to be both green and pale may be difficult, but both terms carry associations. Green is associated with envy and paleness with fear or illness. Meanwhile in the line 'Your spring and your day are wasted in play' one of the most stressed words is 'wasted' – there is a strong suggestion that the joys of childhood are inadequate preparation for being an adult.

The first poem involved aspects of time, but in the second poem time is not only the night and day of a single day but also spring and winter. The symbolic values of spring and winter are obviously significant, spring being a time of growth, winter of death. The final word 'disguise', like 'echoed' in the first version, is not a strong rhyme – it tails off at the end. It is also an ominous word, suggesting things are not as they seem.

In this version, then, there are structural similarities to encourage us to compare the two poems, but at the same time structural difference to make us find contrast.

The joyous debate of the first poem is replaced by a sour voice of experience in the second. 'What is the point of playing when your life turns out like mine?' seems to be what the voice is saying. As usual with first person voices, though, we need to be careful; this constructed voice is not necessarily the author's.

CHAPTER 2, EXERCISE 4

Here are some possible suggestions:

1. How do they sing the songs in *West*? Do they sing them separately, or is it a chaos of noise? How long do they sing for?
2. How do they exit and how long does it take?
3. The gang are described as 'exploding' on to the stage. How is this managed, depending on the size of the stage? How long do they freeze before Les starts talking?
4. From the use of slashes (/) Les appears to be speaking in verse, yet at the same time his speech is a mixture of the demotic and formal – how does this work on stage?
5. There are several references to *Hamlet* in *West*. Do these have to be in any way highlighted for the audience? Does it matter if they do not 'get' them?

CHAPTER 3, EXERCISE 2

There are almost limitless possible answers to this exercise. The suggestions here are starting points for further possible discussion.

Texts 1 and 3

These texts both have a diary format, so in terms of their presentation, their recording of events day by day, they are similar. This diary format involves texts written to be read by others, in other words 'public diaries', unlike the most private of diaries which are not intended for others to read. Text 1, though, is fictional, in that the experience it records has been made up by the author. Look at the dialogue, for example, which reads very much like the dialogue found in a novel. In 'real-life' diaries speech tends to be reported, and not given in such precise detail. This can be compared to Text 3 where Jane's urgent messages about the fire are reported speech.

Helen Fielding has used aspects of the diary genre to create a fictional situation, but has then broken with the genre to add detail to this fictional world. Pepys, on the other hand, is reporting actual events which happened, but doing so within the conventions of the 'public' diary genre. Although it is tempting to say that one diary is fictional and the other non-fictional, there are subtle similarities between these two texts which make such broad labels problematic.

Texts 2 and 6

These can be linked through content; they are both examples of narrators writing about travel into unknown places. Text 2, though, is playing with the genre by creating an imaginary traveller in an imaginary world. The naïve narrator, Gulliver, sees no reason to comment on what he finds there, whereas we the reader are much more suspicious. We know that such a world cannot exist, and that instead it is modelled on our world. These are not tiny men who are leaping and creeping, but representatives of our world, politicians who will do anything to gain office. And so we see that Swift's purpose is to parody travel writing for a satirical purpose.

Bill Bryson, on the other hand, clearly does visit a real place, Durham, but that does not mean that what he says is the definitive truth. Although it is apparently the voice of Bill Bryson himself who narrates the text, this narrative voice is just as much a created voice as Gulliver's. The narrator here is sharp, witty, clever, informal, opinionated – and hopes overall to inform and amuse the reader.

Texts 5 and 8

These two texts both advertise themselves as poems, so in a broad sense they are linked by similarity of form. They are also the only two complete texts in the collection. More significant, though, is the fact that both are poems which contain an element of visual play; if read aloud they would not have the same impact that they have on the page. Both require the reader to work hard at making meanings. Text 5 not only requires you to understand the conventions of text messaging, but also to think about the significance of the last line. Text 8 plays with the notion of the centaur, half horse half man. It breaks convention by its failure to use capital letters, and by its endless repetition. This repetition, though, is not quite as simple as it seems. If you read the poem by stopping at each piece of punctuation rather than at the end of each line, you can find different ways of looking at the poem, while the end does something different again, this time through breaking the pattern of punctuation.

The texts are different, though, in terms of authorship and production. Text 5 is ephemeral (except for the fact that it is printed here), because it was printed in a newspaper and without any named author. Text 8, though, is taken from a poetry anthology of a named poet, deemed to be good enough to have some of his poems 'selected'.

Texts 4 and 7

Both texts are extracts from long narrative poems, which would be one way of linking them through genre. More significantly, though, both poems can be linked, at least initially, by their apparent similarity of intended response. They are both **epic** poems, in that they seek to place great importance on the stories they tell, and so use language to match. Their readers are meant to see that these stories are grand and shocking. To Milton, and to his readers at the time, no event could be more important than the fall of humankind.

There is, though, a catch here. Pope uses similar techniques to Milton, but why? Just for the loss of a piece of hair? Pope here is clearly using the epic form against itself, and so is writing a sort of **mock epic**. By deliberately painting an exaggerated picture, he is suggesting that we can overreact to petty acts; and to make sure that we don't take it seriously, he links dying husbands and dying lapdogs.

What Pope does here is what many comic writers do. He takes a recognised genre and subverts it through parody, using it for comic and perhaps satirical ends. This means that text 7 can be linked with text 2, which is also in a way subverting a genre. The fact that both texts were published within a few years of each other allows them to be linked in genre through time; this was a period when parody and satire were popular forms of writing.

Texts 1 and 9

Both texts involve a single created character talking to themselves. In text 1 the reader is given access to a supposedly private diary. In the case of Edmund in *King Lear*, it depends upon whether the play is being read or seen. If read only, then we have to imagine what this would be like on stage; if seen performed, then we will not have the words in front of us, but only hear them.

In both texts the characters are in a sense introducing themselves. Bridget Jones (or in reality Helen Fielding), in a few words, makes it clear that she is writing a diary and expressing certain attitudes about her life – she is bored, fed up and so on. As readers we collude in a sort of game here: we know the diary is fictional and really written for us, but we are prepared, at least in part, to read it as though it is private. The same applies to Edmund's speech. This time we agree, as an audience, to accept that a character will appear before us and speak aloud his 'thoughts'. Edmund, too, is unhappy with his lot, but his acceptance of nature as his goddess suggests he intends to do something about it.

There is, though, a crucial difference between the two texts. Text 1 exists only in the written form, whereas Text 9 can be performed in many different ways. If Edmund looks up from his letter, walks to the front of the stage, looks at the audience head on and starts to talk, then he is involving the audience in a very particular sort of event.

OTHER POSSIBLE CONNECTIONS

Each of the texts has been compared above with another text. Although these pairings make obvious connections, various others are possible. Some of these are briefly outlined below.

Texts 1, 2 and 9: All these texts have potentially unreliable narrators: Text 1 because the narrator has been created as being rather immature and insecure, Text 2 because the narrator is ploddingly dull in his failure to be amazed by what he sees, and Text 9 because the speaker/narrator is too confident.

A broader, and so less useful category, would simply involve first person narratives, in which case texts 3, 5, 6, and 8 could be added to the list.

Texts 4 and 7, as well as being linked through their epic, can also be broadly linked in that their narrative voice is in the third person. This is again, though, a very broad and not necessarily helpful connection. Pope's undermining of what is said is very different from Milton's seriousness. Nonetheless, both feature women who are in a sense behaving badly.

Texts 4 and 9 can be linked because they are both written in the same poetic form -blank verse.

Texts 1, 2, 4 6, and possibly even **5** and **8** can all be linked as humorous texts, and so have connections through the intended audience response. The sheer number of texts included here, though, suggests that while humour is a useful category in some ways, the fact that it refers to so many texts that are otherwise different makes it another very broad and unspecific category.

Texts 1 and 5 can be linked through their intended audience. Both require a certain knowledge of contemporary cultural references, and so are primarily, though not exclusively, aimed at a younger audience. They can also be linked by the fact that they both first appeared in newspapers.

Texts 3 and 6 can be connected in that they are both autobiographical, recounting so-called 'real lives'. While this can be a useful genre connection, though, 'reality' is a tricky notion that needs handling with care. Both authors have shaped their experience through writing, and in the process in some ways fictionalised it.

CHAPTER 3, EXERCISE 3

The first point to make here is that it is unusual for a book to be advertised in such a way: unusual because books are not usually commercially viable enough to have full-page colour adverts and unusual in that book adverts are usually much more serious than this. Immediately, then, we can assume, even if we do not know the Discworld books that they can be categorised as *popular fiction* and are meant to be *comedies*.

The very fact that this is said to be the 'latest Discworld novel' suggests that the Discworld *series* is itself being seen as a genre – you need to read more than one to get the full point of what is going on. The *author* is well enough known, and has sold enough books in a series for his work to be a genre by itself. His face and his hat on the road sign also suggest that he has an identifiable physical trademark.

The visual scenes on the 'beer can' and the title of the novel both strongly suggest that these books also belong to the wider genre of *fantasy fiction*.

This advert, though, is also playing with another genre, that of various *beer adverts*. The can and the slogan are both obvious clues here, with the usual Castlemaine XXXX replaced by 4ECKS. XXXX is itself a play upon a four-letter word, and 4ECKS sounds like 4X. But the word 'eck' as in the dialect northern phrase 'by eck' used in Boddington's beer adverts, is an English word for surprised wonder. In other words, this book is a good read.

This Englishness, though, is contrasted with the background image of the Australian scene and the reworking of the well-known Heineken and Carlsberg slogans to produce an idea of the whole world. While playing with the various adverts it intertextually echoes, the publishers are making a claim for the universal popularity of their author.

CHAPTER 4, EXERCISE 4

In the extract Robert and Sarah meet just after Robert's cat, Muriel, has died. Due to a misunderstanding, though, Sarah thinks Muriel was Robert's sister, but Robert does not know she is making this mistake.

One way in which the humour works is that the conversation, whose agenda is controlled by Sarah, does not actually mention any reference to her mistaken idea that she is talking about a sister. Robert, taking his lead from Sarah, responds to her questions without mentioning that it is a cat he is talking about. There is a sense that Robert is puzzled by the strength of her response, but he is too polite to challenge her in any forthright way.

Another way in which the humour works is by making the narrative operate almost exclusively from the perspective of the mistaken character, Sarah. Only once, and then very briefly, are we given any added detail about Robert beyond what he says – 'He shrugged, laughing uneasily'. In other words nearly all his speech is presented as free direct speech. We are given more detail about Sarah, though, in the form of direct speech – 'Sarah nodded / Taken aback for a moment, she mumbled / she asked horrified'. As readers we understand that these are all details involved with being puzzled, shocked and surprised, but we also, unlike the characters, know the reasons why.

Beyond the direct speech, though, we are also given access to Sarah's thoughts, but not to Robert's. In two paragraphs the narrative uses a mixture of free indirect thought and indirect thought to show her unease and uncertainty. The first examples come in the opening paragraph of the extract: 'This was not proceeding at all as she had hoped'. By presenting the narrative from Sarah's thoughts, Coe establishes that at this point in the story the reader is going to be following events from Sarah's perspective.

The second examples of presentation of thought come in the paragraph beginning 'How very male, Sarah thought, to be putting on this bluff display of resilience'. Her thoughts extending beyond the specific case to a comment on all men, and her belief that Muriel was as close to Robert as it was possible to be are justifiable within her mistaken world, but are ludicrously extreme for the reader who knows what is really going on.

The internalisation of the narrative from Sarah's point of view, allied to the reader's superior knowledge to the characters, gives the extract its humour.

CHAPTER 4, EXERCISE 6

In the novel, Amis essentially tells the story in chronologically reverse order – in other words the story works backwards and 'ends' at the 'beginning', rather like a film rewinding. Irene has discovered that Tod has an appalling secret in his past.

Although the book is written backwards in terms of time, it is *representing* time going backwards rather than literally going backwards itself – if this were the case the sentences would begin with full stops and question marks. The clever thing that Amis has done here, though, is to construct a conversation which makes 'sense' whichever direction you read it. If you read it from the moment Tod hangs up the phone (i.e. picks it up in real time) and read backwards, you will find a conversation in which Irene threatens to expose Tod with the information she has acquired about him, and he becomes increasingly worried about what she might do. If you read it from the beginning, the conversation still 'works', although this time it is Irene who seems more stressed by the situation. The word 'goodbye', which either begins or ends the conversation takes on a different meaning depending at which end of the conversation it falls. If at the end of the conversation, then Irene is about to put the phone down; if at the beginning, then she is ending their relationship.

The use of free direct speech (i.e. the speaker is not actually identified) helps Amis to produce this double effect. Only three times is attributed direct speech used, and never when Irene is speaking. Each time a question is used, there is a statement both before and after it. Meanwhile, the absence of any thought is another factor in the way this dialogue works.

CHAPTER 4, EXERCISE 7

Although both extracts are third person narratives, the focus in extract A is on what Jenny sees and thinks. Lurie carefully establishes the geography of Jenny's perspective: she is some way from what happens, looking through a window. Using a mixture of free indirect thought – the word *here* shows that we are positioned with Jenny – and indirect thought, the narrative gives us Jenny's thoughts on what has happened, and Jenny's thoughts only. She misunderstands what she sees, and developing the story in her own head, decides she hates her husband.

For the irony of the situation to work on the reader, we need to have seen Jenny's mistaken view before we see the real one. Had the two narratives been reversed, Jenny would simply have been mistaken. The fact that she could be right, until we find out what Wilkie actually thinks, makes the greater impact. The repetition of the same incident twice is an aspect of chronology – time is stopped and replayed.

Extract B focuses on Wilkie's thoughts and perceptions. It starts with free indirect thought, moves towards the scene viewed through his eyes, and then contains direct speech. This variety of methods can be applied because Wilkie is moving towards his home and then is at the centre of the episode; Jenny's view is more static and distant.

The key event, the kiss which causes all the misunderstanding, is seen very much from his perspective – after all, he is on the receiving end of it. The words 'wet, sloppy' suggest it is not a pleasant experience. From his point of view Barbie Mumpson is a nuisance.

While it is not possible to talk about extracts in the same way that you can talk about the whole novel, the reader can make various responses to this episode. The way the narrative has been organised, first through Jenny's perception and then through Wilkie's, means that the reader is in a privileged position over the characters with regard to knowledge. Although at first the reader may have an instinctive sympathy with Jenny, the loyal wife who seems to be being deceived, once we know the situation from Wilkie's point of view too, we are likely to have sympathies with both characters.

This shared sympathy means that with its ironic misunderstandings the reader will probably see the episode overall as comic, yet at the same time there is a sense of sadness that Jenny is missing the point at what the reader knows is such a crucial time. In addition, though, readers are likely to enjoy the way in which Alison Lurie has shaped this narrative. It is not just the plot which makes an effective story; it is the way that plot is presented to the reader.

CHAPTER 5, EXERCISE 4

Pinter's purpose here is to entertain and he presumably intends the audience to be amused. We may feel that we have met people like these two men, even overheard conversations like this, but as with all literature what we are seeing and hearing is a representation of the way some people talk at certain times. Pinter is representing dysfunctional characters whose communication is limited, to say the least, but for all that, his dialogue has a shape to it that is typical of literary representation rather than real-life talk. The patterns of repetition around the name George, the way the men seem to know George and not know him, the sense that they may be talking about a different person are potentially amusing, but nothing like the real-life conversation we have seen. Even Pinter's trademark pauses are artificial: we all have moments of silence, but not in the regular patterns that are here.

Essentially the two men are not listening enough to each other to have a conversation that makes full sense to an audience, and the humour comes from the audience's sense of being puzzled, of not quite being able to work things out. There is also a social class dimension here, and maybe one of gender too – Pinter seems to be representing a stereotype of male working-class speech.

CHAPTER 5, EXERCISE 6

One way to view Benedick's soliloquy is to see it as a character working out his thoughts aloud, rather in the way that people do sometimes talk to themselves in an attempt to reach a conclusion. This gives the playwright the opportunity to look inside Benedick's head, in the way a novelist can by presenting thought. If the soliloquy is taken in this way, the audience overhears what is being said/thought rather than being addressed directly.

The problem with this is that the audience is usually spoken to directly by the actor. In this case Benedick is alone on stage and likely to face the audience. The audience, though, is like all audiences in receipt of a monologue – it is not free to shout back, but merely able to listen. Sometimes an actor might interact with an audience when speaking a soliloquy, by winking, appealing with hands or voice and so on, but although this will bring the audience into a closer relationship with the character, they are still silent (unless, perhaps, they are watching a pantomime, which does allow audiences to shout out).

Part of the humour here stems from Benedick coming to terms with what the audience has already guessed – that he does find Beatrice attractive. The irony that there has indeed been a 'trick' played on Benedick, and that a trick is needed to make him see what everyone else knows is obvious, is seen only by the audience.

Benedick's speech, unlike Beatrice's, is in prose, which allows Shakespeare to build up a whole series of disjointed clauses, with many switches of focus: some looking back on what he has just heard, others looking forward to the future and how he will be looked upon for changing his mind. The effect of this is to suggest a character who is thinking aloud, discovering as he goes.

Beatrice's speech, in verse, is less frantic, beginning not with a statement but with three questions. Who is she talking to when she says, 'Can this be true?' In one sense, herself, but again it would seem obvious that the audience is in part going to feel that they are being asked the question too. It is an ironic effect of the stage soliloquy that the audience can feel very close to a character when the character is behaving in such a particularly unrealistic way.

CHAPTER 5, EXERCISE 7

Regional speech is often represented in the text of plays (and novels too) by marked examples of accent and dialect rather than by fully consistent use. In representing local speech, it is hinted at rather than accurately represented, as local speech by definition is not necessarily accessible to a wide English-speaking audience. So although an actor might well play up the features of a cockney accent, only the dropped aitches on Enry Iggins show that here. All the other 'h' sounds are written in. Similarly with dialect words: 'worrited' could be taken as a dialect form, but the rest of the speech here is in standard English.

Although there is in reality no such thing as speech which belongs exclusively to one social class, in literature working-class speech is often represented in a certain way. Here it is Doolittle's use of 'I says' and 'says I' which suggests that beneath the clothes he has not changed, although 'says I' is hardly typical of working-class speech.

Doolittle has an honesty which his so-called betters do not have and so to that extent, for all his faults, he is superior to them. The fact that he says he was happy in his poverty emphasises the point. This Romantic view of the poor is not necessarily 'true' but it shows one of the ways in which demotic speech is used to make a social point.

CHAPTER 6, EXERCISE 4

1. As was shown in the earlier discussion of metaphors, we frequently use metaphors that are 'inactive'; by being 'lexicalised' they have been defined in dictionaries with their new meanings. All of the following could be seen as metaphorical in origin, but are unlikely to be seen as metaphorical either now, or in 1867. These include:

> The sea is calm
> The tide is full
> the cliffs of England stand
> the tranquil bay
> sweet is the night-air

It could be argued, therefore, that in this first verse none of the language is foregrounded, brought to our attention, by being metaphorical.

2. As with stanza 1, much of the early description such as 'strand', 'grating' and 'fling' could be seen as metaphorical. The term 'moon-blanch'd' – made white by the moon – is a metaphor, but not a particularly unusual one.

The poem moves forward in its ideas, and at the same time uses more striking metaphor in this stanza's last two lines. Arnold gives first a musical metaphor – 'tremulous cadence' – and then takes this a stage further by describing the musical sound as a 'note of sadness'.

3. Having introduced the idea of the sea sounding sad, Arnold says he is not the first person to have thought this – indeed the thought goes right back to the early civilisation of the Greeks. To Sophocles the sound of the sea reminded him of the 'turbid ebb and flow / Of human misery'. Note, though, how clearly Arnold signals the comparison here, by using the words 'it brought / into his mind' and 'we find also'.

4. Unlike the previous two stanzas, this one is packed with images – they are called images because they extend beyond a single descriptive use. The first line, standing alone to highlight it, and using capital letters, is the line upon which the whole poem pivots. The sea which he/we have seen and heard now comes to represent the whole idea of faith in God. This sea was 'once' right up to the shore (i.e. everybody believed) but 'now' it is withdrawing (i.e. some people no longer believe). This withdrawal is personified as 'melancholy' – the loss of faith is a sad experience, not a happy release.

The other main image here is of the personified earth once wearing a 'bright girdle' but now being left 'naked', because the sea of faith has gone.

Effective metaphors work because they give the reader a new way of looking at/understanding something. The more 'applicable' the comparison, the more the reader will see the point. A criticism of this as a comparison of lost faith would be that the sea may be retreating now, but it will come back with the next tide – something which Arnold perhaps overlooks.

5. This verse mixes direct statements with metaphorical language. The word 'seems' introduces a simile about 'a land of dreams', which is then dismissed as being false by the network of similes and metaphors which close the poem. We, that is all humanity, are not at the coast at all, but 'here as on a darkling plain'. This simile of a barren land is made worse by the sense of confusion, noise and warfare conjured up in the last lines. This is not literal war, though, but metaphorical war. One interpretation of this metaphor is that the 'ignorant armies' are ignorant because all the certainty of faith they once had is now gone, they know nothing for sure any more. All that is left to base our lives upon are confused theories which fight each other so we must take refuge in the only truth we can offer each other – love.

6. The poem which began with 'calm tonight' ends with 'armies' and 'night'. This movement of ideas, sounds and mood in the poem has been achieved by a number of methods: the organisation of the poem being one, poetic effects around sound being another. At key points, though, it is metaphorical language which has carried the weight of this argument, with the final lines, because they are metaphorical, allowing a number of possible readings.

CHAPTER 6, EXERCISE 5

The fictional place is the Garden of Love, and it is signalled to the reader through the title and the repetition in the first line. The first change is that a chapel has been built, where the speaker used to 'play'. Associated with this chapel are graves, tombstones and priests in black gowns walking where 'flowers should be'.

The last line adds a metaphor to what is already an allegory. Even within the fictional world of the garden, emotions cannot literally be tied with briars. This, along with the fact that the line is placed at the end of the poem, suggests that it is helping the reader to interpret the poem as a whole.

Allegorical texts, by their very nature, are impossible to pin down with absolute confidence. (Consider the way that religious texts have been endlessly reinterpreted over time.) The final line, though, is a good starting point, because it gives a pretty strong clue that the 'priests in black gowns' are the villains of the story, repressing the natural 'joys and desires' that were previously experienced in the Garden of Love. Although the word 'Love' can be taken in various ways, when linked to 'joys and desires', it would appear that it is sexual repression that the priests are engaged in. The garden was once a place of 'play' and 'flowers' but is now filled with images of death, such as graves and tombstones. Organised religion denies pleasure rather than encouraging it.

The fact that the allegory involves a garden would have reminded many of Blake's readers of the Garden of Eden. This is just one interpretation of the poem, though. There are other possible variations.

CHAPTER 6, EXERCISE 6

One method that Lethem uses involves the organisation of the text, more especially the paragraphing and syntax. The fact that this is all one long paragraph, until Lionel actually screams, suggests a torrent of words waiting to be released. (He actually uses the word 'torrent' near the end of the paragraph.) Although a few of the sentences, like the first two, are brief, the majority are much longer, containing lists piled on top of each other.

Many of these lists contain strings of unusual metaphors, unusual because words, which are abstract things, are personified in an increasingly unexpected and unusual way. So, for example, they are compared to escapees, husks, armies, a flood and so forth. The single most extended metaphor, though, involves the words being like human hands, which play the piano, massage, put hairs in place, replace divots, pat old ladies and so on. While we can just about conceive that massed words are like massed armies, the notion of words patting old ladies gently on the behind is beyond any recognisable connection in the world we know, which is, of course, the whole point – Tourette's syndrome is a condition which those of us fortunate enough not to have it can know little about.

Meanwhile, towards the end of the extract, the urge to shout is described as an itch – an itch which has to be scratched by the fingers of words. He addresses the reader directly, and tells us to 'Cover your ears,' blurring the distinction between a written and a spoken narrative, between what is going on in his head and on the page.

And then the dam bursts and he screams – and what he says is meaningless in any ordinary sense of meaning. He has warned us at the start, though, that 'Context is everything,' so within the context of what we have been told, we do not expect his utterances to be conventionally meaningful.

REFERENCES

Goatly, A. (1977) *The Language of Metaphors*, London: Routledge.
Lakoff, G., and Johnson, M. (1980) *Metaphors We Live by*, Chicago: University of Chicago Press.

GLOSSARY

This is a form of combined glossary and index. Listed below are some of the key terms used in the book, together with brief definitions for purposes of reference. The page references will normally take you to the first use of the term in the book, where it will be shown in bold.

Allusion   When one text makes a reference to another

Characterisation   This refers to the way characters are presented by an author

Chronological narrative   This is when a story is told in the time sequence in which events 'occur'

Cohesion   A term which refers to the patterns of language created within a text, mainly within and across sentence boundaries, and which collectively make up the organisation of larger units of text. Cohesion can be both lexical and grammatical. Lexical cohesion can be established by chains of words of related meaning which link across sentences (see also **semantic field**)

Complex sentence   A sentence made up of a main part and subordinate parts

Compound sentence   A sentence where parts are joined by connectives

Connective   A term to describe words which link linguistic units such as clauses. Words such as 'and', 'but' and 'therefore' are connectives

Context   Literally 'with the text'. Context looks at the circumstances which affect the production of the text by an author and the circumstances which affect the receptions of the text by readers

Demotic   Suggesting language spoken by ordinary people

Discourse   Discourse is used in various ways. It can refer to a continuous piece of written or spoken text, but as used in this book it refers to more than this. Here it refers to the way texts cohere (see **cohesion**) and the ways in which readers recognise this

Dominant reading position   When reading a text we may work out that one particular interpretation is preferred by the author over others. This is known as the dominant reading position (see also **oppositional reading position**)

Dramatisation   The methods used by a playwright to allow a play to be staged

Ephemeral text   A text soon discarded or forgotten

Epic   As used here, this refers to a long narrative poem recounting events of huge significance (see **mock epic**)

Genre and subgenre   Genre refers to an identifiable text-type. It can be used in a number of ways: to identify a type of writing as in a report, a letter, a poem; and it can identify a group of texts which have subject matter in common as in crime fiction, travel writing, sports writing. Subgenre is a branch of a genre, so if the genre is crime fiction, then police procedural is a subgenre

Grammar   The systems by which texts and meanings are constructed

Graphology   This involves analysing how the appearance of a text affects the ways in which it is read and understood

Intertextuality   This refers to the ways in which one text carries echoes or references to other texts

Irony   This is a complex term, but essentially it involves the difference between what is said and what is meant

Lexis   The study of lexis involves looking at a text at the level of its words

Metaphor   A word or a phrase which establishes a comparison or analogy between one object or idea and another. 'The game exploded into life' compares a football game with a bomb, for instance

Metonymy   Metonymy involves replacing the name of something with something that is connected to it, without being the whole thing. For example the President of the United States, his government and advisors, are sometimes replaced by the much simpler term 'The White House', which is the presidential residence and administrative centre. Likewise, 'Number 10 Downing Street', or even just 'Number 10' are often used to refer to the British government

Mock epic   Whereas epic refers to text recounting events of huge significance, mock epic takes trivial events and makes them even more trivial by pretending they are of epic proportions

Narrative persona   The persona is the invented voice which presents a narrative – the 'I' of a narrative which is not necessarily the voice of the author

Narrative voice   The narrative voice is the voice which 'tells' a story. A simple distinction of narrative voice is between **third person** (she/he/they) and **first person** (I) although within these broad categories there are many subtle distinctions.

Narrator, narratee   The narrator is the person in a text who appears to be addressing the reader. The narratee is the implied reader of a text, whose identity is built up by a series of assumptions made about the reader

Oppositional reading position   Although we may recognise a **dominant reading position** (see above), we may nonetheless still wish to take a different view of the text, in which case we take an oppositional reading position

Parody   The imitation of an author's writing or of a specific text, often in order to make a satirical point (see **satire**)

Passive voice   Voice refers to whether the subject of a sentence is the agent of an action (in which case it is active) or is affected by the action, in which case it is passive

Phonology   Aspects of the sound system of language

Pragmatics   The way meanings in texts, written or spoken, can work beyond the apparent surface meaning

Prosody   Prosodic features refer to aspects of sound such as pitch, volume and tempo

Rhetorical question   Rhetoric is a term which broadly describes persuasive language, so a rhetorical question is part of a persuasive technique, in which a speaker asks a question which they do not expect to be answered

Satire   The use of humour to criticise human behaviour

Semantics and semantic field   Semantics refers to the study of linguistic meaning. A semantic field is a group of words related in meaning as a result of being connected with a particular context of use. 'Shot', 'header', 'tackle', 'throw-in' are all connected with the semantic field of football

Soliloquy   Although the Latin derivation of the word soliloquy suggests 'solo speaker', the term is usually defined as the representation of the thoughts of a character being spoken aloud. This, though, is not always the case

Source The original material used and adapted by an author in creating a new text

Speech and thought:
    Direct speech/thought is when the 'actual' words used by a character are presented to the reader.
    Indirect speech/thought is when the words are reported.
    Free speech/thought is when the words are not attributed to anyone.

Syntax The way sentences are constructed

Unreferenced pronoun Once a specific reference has been made to a noun, a pronoun can then be used afterwards; for example 'Pope wrote the poem. He called it an epigram.' ('Pope' is followed by 'he' and 'poem' by 'it'.) Ambiguity can be created by using a pronoun that has no specific reference back to a noun